D1263698

"The documents included in the text ~~~~ ~~ exceptional. They reflect a diversity of sources and perspectives and are introduced pedagogically in a variety of ways."

— T.J. Tomlin, *University of Northern Colorado*

## A variety of sources and perspectives help students appreciate the many ways people experience the past.

True to their plural title, Hewitt and Lawson present an inclusive view of American history that shows how events at the national level, shaped by elite political and economic leaders, directly affect the lives of ordinary people, and how actions at the local level affect decisions made at the centers of national government and commerce. By examining multiple angles of American history, students will better understand how the impact of events means different things to different people and constituent groups.

**New to this Edition**
More coverage of Native Americans, Latinos, Asian Americans, and the West.

## A convenient format at an exceptional value.

By placing the narrative and documents together, the book offers a cost-effective way to purchase course materials—with the added convenience of having everything students need in one place. This value increases through the assessment tools and additional resources in LaunchPad.

**New to this Edition**
A new primary source reader, *Document Projects for Exploring American Histories*, available in LaunchPad or in two printed volumes.

**LaunchPad**
macmillan learning

## NEW in LaunchPad for *Exploring American Histories*

**"Thinking Through Sources" activities extend and amplify the document projects in the new companion reader for the book.** Surrounded by a distinctive and sophisticated pedagogy of auto-graded exercises, these interactive activities guide students in assessing their understanding of the sources, in organizing those sources for use in an essay, and in drawing useful conclusions from them. Designed to build arguments and to practice historical reasoning, this unique pedagogy does for skill development what LearningCurve does for content mastery and reading comprehension.

**New source-based questions in the test bank and LearningCurve** give instructors easier ways to test students on their understanding of sources in the book. Details from images and excerpts from the documents are provided to students for quick reference as they answer the questions.

**Questions in the test bank can now be sorted by chapter learning objectives.** This lets instructors test on portions of chapters and makes it easier to see which major concepts students need help understanding.

LaunchPad's integration of book and online assignments is strong. Its LearningCurve application allows students to immediately test their retention of the material and link back to the specific text if they are unsure, and it provides a means for instructors to monitor the reading and retention of students throughout the course."

— Gabrielle Everett,
*Jefferson College*

# LaunchPad

## Where content counts. Where service matters. Where students learn.

Easy to integrate into a campus LMS, LaunchPad provides smart and fun ways to help students learn about American history. LaunchPad also gives instructors everything *they* need to quickly set up a course, craft presentations and lectures, assign and assess homework, and guide the progress of individual students and the class as a whole. In LaunchPad for *Exploring American Histories*:

**An interactive e-book integrates the text and all student media,** including LearningCurve, primary documents, maps, images, videos, assignments, and activities. It also includes the new companion reader *Document Projects for Exploring American Histories* (also in print), which includes additional document projects for assignment.

**LearningCurve.** Tired of your students not reading the textbook? Assign LearningCurve in LaunchPad, and the system's analytics will show what your students have read and understood before they come to class. Each chapter-based activity gives students multiple chances to understand key concepts, consult the narrative textbook if needed, and answer questions correctly. Over 90% of students report satisfaction with LearningCurve's fun and accessible game-like interface.

The **Video Assignment Tool** makes it easy to assign, submit, and assess video-based coursework.

**LaunchPad's Gradebook** gives a clear window on performance for the whole class, for individual students, and for individual assignments.

**Pre-built chapter units,** can be assigned quickly as is or easily customized with additional LaunchPad resources or an instructor's own material. Instructors also may choose to build a course entirely from scratch. Pre-built units include pages from the textbook and companion reader, LearningCurve, guided reading activities, primary source quizzes, and summative quizzes.

| Instructor Resources include | Student Resources include |
| --- | --- |
| Instructor's Resource Manual | Additional Primary Sources |
| Test Bank | Videos (historical film) |
| The Bedford Lecture Kit Presentation Slides | Flashcards |
| Maps and Images (jpeg and presentation slide formats) | Timeline Activities |
| Outline Maps | Map Quizzes |

## launchpadworks.com  •  learningcurveworks.com

# How to Use This Book

Point your students to the chapter tools to help them focus on what's important as they read.

**Learning Objectives** preview what is important to take away from each section of the chapter.

A pair of **American Histories biographies** at the start of each chapter personalize the history of the period, and the narrative touches upon these stories throughout to bring history to life.

At the end of each major section and repeated in the chapter review, the **Review & Relate questions** review key concepts.

---

## LEARNING **OBJECTIVES**

After reading this chapter you should be able to:

- Analyze the ways that social and cultural leaders worked to craft an American identity and how that was complicated by racial, ethnic, and class differences.

- Interpret how the Democratic-Republican ideal of limiting federal power was transformed by international events, westward expansion, and Supreme Court rulings between 1800 and 1808.

- Explain the ways that technology reshaped the American economy and the lives of distinct groups of Americans.

## AMERICAN HISTORIES

When Parker Cleaveland graduated from Harvard University in 1799, his parents expected him to pursue a career in medicine, law, or the ministry. Instead, he turned to teaching. In 1805 Cleaveland secured a position in Brunswick, Maine, as professor of mathematics and natural philosophy at Bowdoin College. A year later, he married Martha Bush. Over the next twenty years, the Cleavelands raised eight children on the Maine frontier, entertained visiting scholars, corresponded with families at other colleges, and boarded dozens of students. While Parker taught those students math and science, Martha trained them in manners and morals. The Cleavelands also

*(left)* **Parker Cleaveland.** Courtesy the Bowdoin College Library, Brunswick, Maine, USA

*(right)* **Shoshone woman.** (No image of Sacagawea exists.) Joslyn Museum, Omaha, Nebraska, USA/Alecto Historical Editions/Bridgeman Images

242

*Copyright © Bedfo[rd]*

served as a model of new ideals of companionate marriage, in which husbands and wives shared interests and affection.

Professor Cleaveland believed in using scientific research to benefit society. When Brunswick workers asked him to identify local rocks, Parker began studying geology and chemistry. In 1816 he published his *Elementary Treatise on Mineralogy and Geology*, providing a basic text for students and interested adults. He also lectured throughout New England, displaying mineral samples and performing chemical experiments.

The Cleavelands viewed the Bowdoin College community as a laboratory in which distinctly American values and ideas could be developed and sustained. So, too, did the residents of other college towns. Although less than 1 percent of men in the United States attended universities at the time, frontier colleges were considered important vehicles for bringing virtue—especially the desire to act for the public good—to the far reaches of the early republic. Yet several of these colleges were constructed with the aid of slave labor, and all were built on land bought or confiscated from Indians.

The purchase of the Louisiana Territory by President Thomas Jefferson in 1803 marked a new American frontier and ensured further encroachments on native lands. The territory covered 828,000 square miles and stretched from the Mississippi River to the Rocky Mountains and from New Orleans to present-day Montana. The area was home to tens of thousands of Indian inhabitants.

In the late 1780s, a daughter, later named Sacagawea, was born to a family of Shoshone Indians who lived in an area that became part of the Louisiana Purchase. In 1800 she was taken captive by a Hidatsa raiding party. Sacagawea and her fellow captives were marched hundreds of miles to a Hidatsa-Mandan village on the Missouri River. Eventually Sacagawea was sold to a French trader, Toussaint Charbonneau, along with another young Shoshone woman, and both became his wives.

In November 1804, an expedition led by Meriwether Lewis and William Clark set up winter camp near the Hidatsa village where Sacagawea lived. The U.S. government sent Lewis and Clark to document

from the dangers embedded in the nation's oppressive racial history.

## REVIEW & RELATE

◆ How did new inventions and infrastructure improvements contribute to the development of the American economy?

◆ Why did slavery expand and become mor[e] deeply entrenched in southern society in the early nineteenth century? What fears did this reinforce?

---

Use the integrated, stepped approach to primary sources to strengthen students' interpretive skills while bringing history to life.

## Step 1: Guided Analysis

Near the start of each chapter, a **Guided Analysis** of a textual or visual source with annotating questions in the margins model how to analyze a specific phrase or detail of the source as well as the source as a whole.

**Red Explore callouts** in the narrative highlight the connections between the narrative and specific sources and help students move easily to the sources and back.

**Explore ▶**

See Document 22.1 for a letter from the Scottsboro prisoners.

---

### GUIDED ANALYSIS

#### Plea from the Scottsboro Prisoners, 1932

In 1931, nine black youths were arrested in Scottsboro, Alabama, and charged with raping two white women. They were quickly convicted, and eight were sentenced to death. (One of the nine, Roy Wright, was twelve years old, and the prosecution did not seek the death penalty.) In this letter to the editor of the *Negro Worker*, a Communist magazine, the Scottsboro Nine plead their innocence and ask for help. A year had passed since their arrest and trial, which would account for their ages in the following statement recorded as between thirteen to twenty. Only those sentenced to death signed the letter.

**Document 22.1**

*Why do you think they mention their ages?*

*What tactics did Alabama officials use on the prisoners? What was their purpose?*

*Why do the Scottsboro prisoners repeatedly emphasize that they were workers?*

We have been sentenced to die for something we ain't never done. Us poor boys have been sentenced to burn up on the electric chair for the reason that we is workers—and the color of our skin is black. We like any one of you workers is none of us older than 20. Two of us is 14 and one is 13 years old.

What we guilty of? Nothing but being out of a job. Nothing but looking for work. Our kinfolk was starving for food. We wanted to help them out. So we hopped a freight—just like any one of you workers might a done—to go down to Mobile to hunt work. We was taken off the train by a mob and framed up on rape charges.

At the trial they gave us in Scottsboro we could hear the crowd yelling, "Lynch the Niggers." We could see them toting those big shotguns. Call 'at a fair trial? And while we lay here in jail, the boss-man make us watch 'em burning up other Negroes on the electric chair. "This is what you'll get," they say to us.

Working class boys, we asks you to save us from being burnt on the electric chair. We's only poor working class boys whose skin is black. . . . Help us boys. We ain't done nothing wrong.

[Signed] Andy Wright, Olen Montgomery, Ozie Powell, Charlie Weems, Clarence Norris, Haywood Patterson, Eugene Williams, Willie Robertson

Source: "Scottsboro Boys Appeal from Death Cells to the 'Toilers of the World,'" *The Negro Worker* 2, no. 5 (May 1932): 8–9.

**Put It in Context**

Why was it unlikely that black men in Alabama could receive a fair trial on the charge of raping a white woman?

---

legal representation and
the jury pool. Although
dence of r:
time the d
ing the ch:
of whom l
this racist

## Step 2: Comparative Analysis

Next, each chapter progresses to the more complex **Comparative Analysis**—a paired set of documents that reveal contrasting or complementary perspectives on a particular issue.

---

**COMPARATIVE ANALYSIS**

### Letters to Eleanor Roosevelt

During the 1930s Americans wrote to President Roosevelt and the First Lady in unprecedented numbers, revealing their personal desperation and their belief that the Roosevelts would respond to their individual pleas. Though most requested government assistance, not all letter writers favored the New Deal. In the following letters written to Eleanor Roosevelt, a high school girl from Albertville, Alabama, asks the First Lady for personal help, while Minnie Hardin of Columbus, Indiana, expresses her frustration with direct relief programs.

**Document 22.2**

#### Mildred Isbell to Mrs. Roosevelt, January 1, 1936

Dear Mrs. Roosevelt,

My life has been a story to me and most of the time a miserable one. When I was 7 years old my father left for a law school and never returned. This leaving my mother and 4 children. He left us a small farm, but it could not keep us up. For when we went back to mother's people the renters would not give us part, and we were still dependent. I have been shoved to pillar to post that I feel very

I am now 15 ye[...] have always been s[...] as all of us is so poo[...] education, but I will[...] there is no clothes o[...] that we are on the r[...] faithful servent for [...] see how she has ma[...]

Mrs Roosevelt, don't think I am just begging, but that is all you can call it I guess. There is no harm in asking I guess eather. Do you have any old clothes you have throwed back. You don't realize how honored I would feel to be wearing your clothes. I don't have a coat at all to wear. The clothes may be too large but I can cut them down so I can wear them. Not only clothes but old shoes, hats, hose, and under wear would be [...]

Sources: Mildred Isbell, letter to [...]
Eleanor Roosevelt Papers, Serie[...]

**Document 22.3**

#### Minnie Hardin to Mrs. Roosevelt, December 14, 1937

Mrs. Roosevelt:

I suppose from your point of view the work relief, old age pensions, slum clearance, and all the rest seems like a perfect remedy for all the ills of this country, but I would like for you to see the results, as the other half see them.

We have always had a shiftless, never-do-well class of people whose one and only aim in life is to live without work. I have been rubbing elbows with this class for nearly sixty years and have tried to help some of the most promising and have seen others try to help them, but it can't be done. We cannot help those who will not try to help themselves and if they do try, a square deal is all they need, and by the way that is all this country needs or ever has needed: a square deal

for all and then, let each paddle their own canoe, or sink.

There has never been any necessity for any one who is able to work, being on relief in this locality, but there have been many eating the bread of charity and they have lived better than ever before. I have had taxpayers tell me that their children came from school and asked why they couldn't have nice lunches like the children on relief. The women and children around here have had to work at the fields to help save the crops and several women fainted while at work and at the same time we couldn't go up or down the road without stumbling over some of the reliefers, moping around carrying dirt from one side of the road to the other and back again, or else asleep.

**Interpret the Evidence**

1. How does each writer explain the source of poverty and the attitudes of poor people?
2. If Minnie Hardin were answering Mildred Isbell's letter, what would she say to her?

**Put It in Context**

How did the New Deal tackle poverty?

---

Visit **macmillanlearning.com/requesthewitt2e** for more information, review copy requests, and custom solutions. Or contact your local Macmillan Learning Representative.

Near the end of each chapter, students encounter a **Solo Analysis**—a single document that encourages further practice working with sources without the aid of annotations or a comparative source to focus interpretation.

**Interpret the Evidence questions** help students analyze the sources.

A **Put It in Context question** at the end of each source feature helps students connect primary sources to the larger historical narrative.

### SOLO ANALYSIS

**Retire or Move Over, 1937**

In his first term, President Roosevelt secured legislation to implement his New Deal; however, by 1937 the Supreme Court had overturned several key pieces of New Deal legislation, arguing that Congress had exceeded its constitutional authority. As the Social Security Act and the National Labor Relations Act came up for review before the Court, Roosevelt tried to dilute the influence of the Court's conservative majority. Following his landslide reelection in 1936, he asked Congress to enlarge the Court so that he could appoint justices more favorable to his liberal agenda. This cartoon reacts to Roosevelt's court-packing plan.

**Document 22.4**

Granger, NYC

**Interpret the Evidence**

1. How does the cartoonist portray Roosevelt? How does it portray the Supreme Court?
2. How does this cartoon appeal to the fears of the American public during the late 1930s?

**Put It in Context**

How important was the Supreme Court in shaping the outcome of the New Deal?

Finally, to give students the opportunity to draw deeper conclusions, a **Document Project** of 4-5 sources focused on a central topic concludes each chapter.

## DOCUMENT PROJECT 8

# The Corps of Discovery: Paeans to Peace and Instruments of War

From 1804 to 1806, the Corps of Discovery mapped vast regions of the West, documented plants and animals, and initiated trade relations with Indian nations. When the Corps built its winter camp at Fort Mandan in October 1804, its members hoped to develop commercial relations with local Mandan, Hidatsa, and Arikara villages. Most of these tribes had been ravaged by smallpox in the early 1780s and were now subject to raids by more powerful nations in the region. Meriwether Lewis and William Clark hoped to persuade all of these nations that peaceful relations would benefit them politically and economically. To aid negotiations, the Corps offered gifts to the Indian leaders they encountered (Document 8.5). The Mandan, however, expected more gifts than the expedition could offer. Although Lewis and Clark assured Mandan leaders they would benefit from future trade with and protection from the United States, the Indians had heard such promises before and were wary of giving away vital food as winter descended (Document 8.6).

Worried about surviving the winter, Lewis and Clark finally found an unexpected item to trade with the Mandan. When their men finished building a smithy in December 1804, they discovered that Indians would exchange almost any item for metal hatchets, especially those des[...] uments 8.7 and 8.8).

In April the Corps move[...] day Idaho and traded with S[...] horses. The Shoshone were e[...] lucrative trade in horses. The[...] had split from the Shoshone[...] developed ties with the Spani[...]

270
Copyright © Bedford/St. Martin's.

had a harder time getting guns, a concern [...] expressed to Lewis (Document 8.9). While Lewi[...] Clark advocated peace among Indian nations, o[...] their most desired trade items was weaponry. [...] their explorations inspired white settlement i[...] vast western territory, that weaponry would bec[...] more important than ever.

### Document 8.5

**William Clark, Journal** | **October 12, 1804**

As the Corps of Discovery traveled up the Misso[...] River from St. Louis, they stopped at Indian villa[...] along the way to advocate peace; offer presents [...] President Jefferson; and learn about local plants [...] animals, and potential trade items. In his journal [...] entry for October 12, William Clark describes a v[...] to a Ricara (Arikara) village near where the Corps[...] planned to stay for the winter.

After breakfast, we went on shore to the house of the chief of the second village named Lassel, where we found his chief[...] and warriors. They made us a present of about se[...] bushels of corn, a pair of leggings, a twist of their[...] tobacco, and the seeds of two different species of[...] tobacco. The chief then delivered a speech expressive of his gratitude for the presents and the good [...]ven him; his intention of [...]e president of the United [...]Sioux; and requested us to [...]efs up to the Mandans and [...]n the two nations. . . . A[...]lained the magnitude a[...]s, the three chiefs cam[...]em some sugar, a little [...]em left us, and the chie[...]

### Document 8.6

**Charles McKenzie** | **Narrative of a Fur Trader, November 1804**

Charles McKenzie was a Scotsman working as a clerk for the Hudson Bay Company. He arrived with six traders at a Hidatsa village in November 1804. Over time, McKenzie adopted Indian dress, married an Indian woman, and became an advocate for Indian concerns. Here he recounts Lewis's frustration in his efforts to gain favor with local Indians as well as Mandan concerns about the Corps' lack of generosity.

Here we also found a party of forty Americans under the command of Captains Lewis and Clark exploring a passage by the Mississippi [Missouri] to the Pacific Ocean—they came up the River in a Boat of twenty oars accompanied by two

### Document 8.8

**William Clark** | **Journal, January 28, 1805, and Meriwether Lewis, Journal, February 1, 1805**

By early 1805 it was clear to Lewis and Clark that metal goods, especially axes or hatchets, were the most valuable means of obtaining the corn and other items they needed from the Mandans and neighboring Indians. These two short entries, by Clark and then Lewis, describe the value of the trade in hatchets to the Corps and their continued commitment to peace among Indian nations.

### Document 8.7

**William Clark** | **Journal, November 18, 1804**

By November 1804, the Corps had built and settled into Fort Mandan, at the convergence of the Missouri and Knife Rivers, for the winter. Lewis and Clark became increasingly aware that their trade with particular groups, like the Mandans, might shift the balance of power in the region. But given the extended journey ahead, they were limited in what goods they could give or trade with local Indians even as they sought to reassure them of U.S. support.

[...]ducts. Not for redistributi[...]

Assign the Chapter Review to help students identify significant historical developments and how they fit together over time.

Encourage students to review the **Timeline of Events**, which shows the relationship among chapter events.

Recommend students study the **Key Terms** list to see if they can define each term and describe its significance.

Ask students to answer the **Review & Relate questions**, which prompt them to recall major concepts in each section.

## TIMELINE OF EVENTS

| | |
|---|---|
| **1931** | Scottsboro Nine tried for rape |
| **1932–1939** | Dust Bowl storms |
| **1932** | Reconstruction Finance Corporation created |
| | River Rouge autoworkers' strike |
| | Farm Holiday Association formed |
| | Bonus Army marches |
| **1933** | Roosevelt moves to stabilize banking and financial systems |
| | Agricultural Adjustment Act passed |
| | Federal Emergency Relief Administration created |
| | Tennessee Valley Authority created |
| | National Recovery Administration created |
| | Civilian Conservation Corps created |
| **1934** | Indian Reorganization Act passed |
| | Francis Townsend forms Old-Age Revolving Pensions Corporation |
| | Huey Long establishes Share Our Wealth movement |
| | Securities and Exchange Commission created |
| **1935** | Charles E. Coughlin organizes National Union for Social Justice |
| | Works Progress Administration created |
| | Social Security Act passed |
| | National Labor Relations Act passed |
| | Congress of Industrial Organizations founded |
| **1937** | Sit-down strike against General Motors |
| | Roosevelt proposes to increase the size of the Supreme Court |
| **1938** | Fair Labor Standards Act passed |

## KEY TERMS

Scottsboro Nine, *723*
Bonus Army, *728*
New Deal, *730*
Federal Deposit Insurance Corporation (FDIC), *730*
Agricultural Adjustment Act, *730*
Tennessee Valley Authority (TVA), *731*
National Recovery Administration (NRA), *731*
Civilian Conservation Corps (CCC), *733*
Works Progress Administration (WPA), *737*
Social Security Act, *738*
National Labor Relations Act, *739*
sit-down strike, *741*
Fair Labor Standards Act, *741*
Indian Reorganization Act (IRA), *742*
court-packing plan, *743*
conservative coalition, *743*

## REVIEW & RELATE

1. How did President Hoover respond to the problems and challenges created by the Great Depression?
2. How did different segments of the American population experience the depression?
3. What steps did Roosevelt take to stimulate economic recovery and provide relief to impoverished Americans during his first term in office?
4. What criticisms did Roosevelt's opponents level against the New Deal?
5. Why and how did the New Deal shift to the left in 1934 and 1935?
6. Despite the president's landslide victory in 1936, why did the New Deal stall during Roosevelt's second term in office?

# Contents

## Exploring American Histories

A History with Sources
Second Edition

The Combined Volume includes all chapters.

Volume 1 includes Chapters 1–14

Volume 2 includes Chapters 14–29

"The best new approach I have seen in a U.S. history survey textbook in some time."

— Donald R. Shaffer, *American Public University System*

> Students tell me this book has helped make history real for them."
>
> — Lacey Holley-McCann, *Columbia State University*

**Chapter 14 is the final chapter of Volume 1 and the beginning chapter of Volume 2.**

> A well written survey of American History that enriches the learning experience with the targeted use of primary sources."
>
> —Carole Lester, *University of Texas at Dallas*

> The writing style is very approachable, and should have broad appeal across college campuses."
>
> — **Gregory Culver,** *Austin Peay State University*

> A visual, well written text that is easy to read and entertaining. It has depth and substance but doesn't overwhelm with too much detail, yet it offers a diversity of perspectives. The primary sources are varied and used well. This book is very good for teaching primary source analysis."
>
> — Linda Upham-Bornstein, *Plymouth State University*

> This textbook is just challenging enough for our community college students and easily adaptable to fully engage our more gifted students in critical thought. I highly recommend this book."
>
> — Gary Donato, *Massachusetts Bay Community Collegey*

> Students like this book because it is intellectually engaging. They all find the book refreshing compared to the textbooks they used in high school and in other college history courses. They also like the fact that the chapters are relatively short, and I like the fact that despite being short, the book is not short on substance."
>
> — Ramon C. Veloso, *Palomar College*

# The Early Republic

## 1790–1820

## WINDOW TO THE PAST

### William Clark, Journal, January 28, 1805

William Clark kept a detailed journal of the 1804–1806 expedition he and Meriwether Lewis led to explore the American West. They were aided by many different Indian groups, especially the Mandan Indians along the Missouri River. They camped near the Mandan in the winter of 1804, before heading into the Rocky Mountains. Here Clark draws a Mandan war hatchet, which was crucial to the tribe's defense.

▶ To discover more about what this primary source can show us, see Document 8.8 on page 292.

American Philosophical Society

After reading this chapter you should be able to:

- Analyze the ways that social and cultural leaders worked to craft an American identity and how that was complicated by racial, ethnic, and class differences.

- Interpret how the Democratic-Republican ideal of limiting federal power was transformed by international events, westward expansion, and Supreme Court rulings between 1800 and 1808.

- Explain the ways that technology reshaped the American economy and the lives of distinct groups of Americans.

## AMERICAN HISTORIES

When Parker Cleaveland graduated from Harvard University in 1799, his parents expected him to pursue a career in medicine, law, or the ministry. Instead, he turned to teaching. In 1805 Cleaveland secured a position in Brunswick, Maine, as professor of mathematics and natural philosophy at Bowdoin College. A year later, he married Martha Bush. Over the next twenty years, the Cleavelands raised eight children on the Maine frontier, entertained visiting scholars, corresponded with families at other colleges, and boarded dozens of students. While Parker taught those students math and science, Martha trained them in manners and morals. The Cleavelands also

served as a model of new ideals of companionate marriage, in which husbands and wives shared interests and affection.

Professor Cleaveland believed in using scientific research to benefit society. When Brunswick workers asked him to identify local rocks, Parker began studying geology and chemistry. In 1816 he published his *Elementary Treatise on Mineralogy and Geology*, providing a basic text for students and interested adults. He also lectured throughout New England, displaying mineral samples and performing chemical experiments.

The Cleavelands viewed the Bowdoin College community as a laboratory in which distinctly American values and ideas could be developed and sustained. So, too, did the residents of other college towns. Although less than 1 percent of men in the United States attended universities at the time, frontier colleges were considered important vehicles for bringing virtue—especially the desire to act for the public good—to the far reaches of the early republic. Yet several of these colleges were constructed with the aid of slave labor, and all were built on land bought or confiscated from Indians.

The purchase of the Louisiana Territory by President Thomas Jefferson in 1803 marked a new American frontier and ensured further encroachments on native lands. The territory covered 828,000 square miles and stretched from the Mississippi River to the Rocky Mountains and from New Orleans to present-day Montana. The area was home to tens of thousands of Indian inhabitants.

In the late 1780s, a daughter, later named Sacagawea, was born to a family of Shoshone Indians who lived in an area that became part of the Louisiana Purchase. In 1800 she was taken captive by a Hidatsa raiding party. Sacagawea and her fellow captives were marched hundreds of miles to a Hidatsa-Mandan village on the Missouri River. Eventually Sacagawea was sold to a French trader, Toussaint Charbonneau, along with another young Shoshone woman, and both became his wives.

In November 1804, an expedition led by Meriwether Lewis and William Clark set up winter camp near the Hidatsa village where Sacagawea lived. The U.S. government sent Lewis and Clark to document

(*left*) **Parker Cleaveland.** Courtesy the Bowdoin College Library, Brunswick, Maine, USA

(*right*) **Shoshone woman.** (No image of Sacagawea exists.) Joslyn Museum, Omaha, Nebraska, USA/Alecto Historical Editions/Bridgeman Images

**242**

flora and fauna in the Louisiana Territory, enhance trade, and explore routes to the Northwest. Charbonneau, who spoke French and Hidatsa, and Sacagawea, who spoke several Indian languages, joined the expedition as interpreters in April 1805.

The only woman in the party, Sacagawea traveled with her infant son strapped to her back. Although no portraits of her exist, her presence was crucial, as Clark noted in his journal: "The Wife of Chabono our interpreter we find reconsiles all the Indians, as to our friendly intentions." Sacagawea did help persuade Indian leaders to assist the expedition, but her extensive knowledge of the terrain and fluency in Indian languages were equally important. ■

The American histories of both Parker Cleaveland and Sacagawea aided the development of the United States. Cleaveland gained fame as part of a generation of intellectuals who symbolized Americans' ingenuity. Although Sacagawea was not considered learned, her understanding of Indian languages and western geography was crucial to Lewis and Clark's success. Like many other Americans, Sacagawea and Cleaveland forged new identities as the young nation developed. Still, racial, class, and gender differences made it impossible to create a single American identity. At the same time, Democratic-Republican leaders sought to shape a new national identity by promising to limit federal power and enhance state authority and individual rights. Instead, western expansion, international crises, and Supreme Court decisions ensured the expansion of federal power.

# The **Dilemmas** of **National Identity**

In his inaugural address in March 1801, President Thomas Jefferson argued that the vast distance between Europe and the United States was a blessing, allowing Americans to develop their own unique culture and institutions. For many Americans, education offered one means of ensuring a distinctive national identity. Public schools could train American children in republican values, while the wealthiest among them could attend private academies and colleges. Newspapers, sermons, books, magazines, and other printed works could also help forge a common identity among the nation's far-flung citizens. Even the presence of Indians and Africans contributed to art and literature that were uniquely American. In addition, the construction of a new capital city to house the federal government offered a potent symbol of nationhood.

Yet these developments also illuminated political and racial dilemmas in the young nation. The decision to move the U.S. capital south from Philadelphia was prompted by concerns among southern politicians about the power of northern economic and political elites. The very construction of the capital, in which enslaved and free workers labored side by side, highlighted racial and class differences. Educational opportunities differed by race and class as well as by sex. How could a singular notion of American identity be forged in a country where differences of race, class, and sex loomed so large?

**Education for a New Nation.**  The desire to create a specifically American culture began as soon as the Revolution ended. In 1783 Noah Webster, a schoolmaster, declared that "America must be as independent in *literature as in Politics*, as famous for *arts* as for

**New England Grammar School** In this New England grammar school in the 1790s, boys and girls gather for instruction by their schoolmaster. They likely used one of Noah Webster's spellers or readers. The schoolmaster taught lessons in geography, as can be seen by the wall map and the two globes at the rear of the room. Granger, NYC

*arms*." To promote his vision, Webster published the *American Spelling Book* (1810) and the *American Dictionary of the English Language* (1828). Webster's books were widely used in the nation's expanding network of schools and academies and led to more standardized spelling and pronunciation of commonly used words.

Before the Revolution, public education for children was widely available in New England and the Middle Atlantic region. In the South, only those who could afford private schooling—perhaps 25 percent of the boys and 10 percent of the girls—received any formal instruction. Few young people enrolled in high school in any part of the colonies. Following the Revolution, state and national leaders proposed ambitious plans for public education, and in 1789 Massachusetts became the first state to demand that each town provide free schools for local children, though attendance policies were decided by the towns.

The American colonies boasted nine colleges that provided higher education for young men, including Harvard, Yale, King's College (Columbia), Queen's College (Rutgers), and the College of William and Mary. After independence, many Americans worried that these institutions were tainted by British and aristocratic influences. New colleges based on republican ideals needed to be founded.

Frontier towns offered opportunities for colleges to enrich the community and benefit the nation. The relative isolation of these villages ensured that students would focus on education. And frontier colleges provided opportunities for ethnic and religious groups outside the Anglo-American mainstream—like Scots-Irish Presbyterians—to cement their place in American society. The young nation benefited as well, albeit at the expense of Indians and their lands. For example, the founding of Franklin College in Athens, Georgia, encouraged white settlement in the state's interior, an area still largely populated by the Creek and Cherokee.

Frontier colleges were organized as community institutions composed of extended families, where administrators, faculty, and their wives guided students, hosted social events, and hired local workers, including servants and slaves. Women were viewed as exemplars of virtue in the new nation, and professors' wives served as maternal figures for young adults away from home. Families of modest means could send their sons to these less expensive colleges, depending on faculty couples to expand their intellect and provide moral guidance. In some towns, students at local female academies joined college men at chaperoned events to cultivate proper relations between the sexes.

### Literary and Cultural Developments.

Older universities also contributed to the development of a national identity. A group known as the Hartford Wits, most of them Yale graduates, gave birth to a new literary tradition. Its members identified mainly as Federalists and published paeans to democracy, satires about Shays's Rebellion, and plays about the proper role of the central government in a republican nation.

A number of novelists emerged in the early republic as well. Advances in printing and the manufacture of paper increased the circulation of novels, a literary genre developed in Britain and continental Europe at the turn of the eighteenth century. Improvements in girls' education then produced a growing audience for novels among women. Authors like Susanna Rowson and Charles Brockden Brown sought to educate readers about virtuous action by placing ordinary women and men in moments of high drama that tested their moral character. Novelists also emphasized new marital ideals, by which husbands and wives became partners and companions in creating a home and family.

Washington Irving became a well-known literary figure in the early republic. He wrote a series of popular folktales, including "The Legend of Sleepy Hollow" and "Rip Van Winkle," that were published in his *Sketchbook* in 1820. They drew on the Dutch culture of the Hudson valley region and often poked fun at more celebratory tales of early American history. In one serious essay, Irving challenged popular accounts of colonial wars that ignored courageous actions by Indians while applauding white atrocities.

Still, books that glorified the nation's past were also enormously popular. Among the most influential were the three-volume *History of the Revolution* (1805) written by Mercy Otis Warren and the *Life of Washington* (1806), a celebratory if fanciful biography by Mason Weems. The influence of American authors increased as residents in both urban and rural areas purchased growing numbers of books.

Artists, too, devoted considerable attention to historical themes. Charles Willson Peale painted Revolutionary generals while serving in the Continental Army and became best known for his portraits of George Washington. Samuel Jennings offered a more radical perspective on the nation's character by incorporating women and African Americans into works like *Liberty Displaying the Arts and Sciences* (1792). Engravings, which were

**Explore ▶**

See Document 8.1 for one artist's image of republican education.

less expensive than paintings, also circulated widely. Many highlighted national symbols like flags, eagles, and Lady Liberty or uniquely American flora and fauna. William Bartram, the son of a botanist, journeyed through the southeastern United States and Florida, and published beautiful illustrations of plants and animals in his *Travels* (1791).

In 1780, the Massachusetts legislature established the American Academy of Arts and Sciences to promote American literature and science. Six years later, Philadelphia's American Philosophical Society created the first national prize for scientific endeavor. Philadelphia was also home to the nation's first medical college, founded at the University of Pennsylvania. Frontier colleges like Bowdoin also promoted new scientific discoveries. As in the arts, American scientists built on developments in continental Europe and Britain but prided themselves on contributing their own expertise.

### The Racial Limits of an American Culture.

American Indians received significant attention from writers and scientists. White Americans in the early republic often wielded native names and symbols as they sought to create a distinct national identity. Some Americans, including whiskey rebels, followed in the tradition of the Boston Tea Party, dressing as Indians to protest economic and political tyranny (see "The Whiskey Rebellion" in Chapter 7). But more affluent whites also embraced Indian names and symbols. Tammany societies, which promoted patriotism and republicanism in the late eighteenth century, were named after a mythical Delaware chief called Tammend. They attracted large numbers of lawyers, merchants, and skilled artisans.

Poets, too, focused on American Indians. In his 1787 poem "Indian Burying Ground," Philip Freneau offered a sentimental portrait that highlighted the lost heritage of a nearly extinct native culture in New England. The theme of lost cultures and heroic (if still savage) Indians became even more pronounced in American poetry in the following decades. Such sentimental portraits of American Indians were less popular along the nation's frontier, where Indians continued to fight for their lands and rights.

Sympathetic depictions of Africans and African Americans by white artists and authors appeared even less frequently. Most were produced in the North and were intended for the rare patrons who opposed slavery. Typical images of blacks and Indians were far more demeaning. When describing Indians in frontier regions, white Americans generally focused on their savagery and their duplicity. Most images of Africans and African Americans exaggerated their perceived physical and intellectual differences from whites, to imply an innate inferiority.

Whether their depictions were realistic, sentimental, or derogatory, Africans, African Americans, and American Indians were almost always presented to the American public through the eyes of whites. Educated blacks like the Reverend Richard Allen of Philadelphia or the Reverend Thomas Paul of Boston wrote mainly for black audiences or corresponded privately with sympathetic whites. Similarly, cultural leaders among American Indians worked mainly within their own nations either to maintain traditional languages and customs or to introduce their people to Anglo-American ideas and beliefs.

The improved educational opportunities available to white Americans generally excluded blacks and Indians. Most southern planters had little desire to teach their slaves to read and write. Even in the North, states did not generally incorporate black children into their plans for public education. African Americans in cities with large free black

## GUIDED ANALYSIS

### Samuel Jennings | Liberty Displaying the Arts and Sciences, 1792

Samuel Jennings was born in Philadelphia and attended the College of Philadelphia before the Revolution. He taught drawing and painted portraits before moving to London to study with Benjamin West in 1787. There his allegorical paintings were exhibited at the Royal Academy. Jennings painted this image for the newly established Library Company of Philadelphia, many of whose directors were Quakers who opposed slavery. The directors requested that he include Lady Liberty with her cap on the end of a pole.

**Document 8.1**

The Library Company of Philadelphia

| Which arts and sciences are displayed in this painting? | What does the broken chain at the feet of Lady Liberty indicate? | What distinguishes the black people inside and outside the building? |

**Put It in Context**

What does this painting suggest about how Jennings and the Library Company directors envisioned American identities in the early republic?

populations established the most long-lived schools for their race. The Reverend Allen opened a Sunday school for children in 1795 at his African Methodist Episcopal Church, and other free blacks formed literary and debating societies. Still, only a small percentage of African Americans received an education equivalent to that available to whites in the early republic.

U.S. political leaders were more interested in the education of American Indians, but government officials left their schooling to religious groups. Several denominations sent missionaries to the Seneca, Cherokee, and other tribes, and a few successful students were then sent to American colleges to be trained as ministers or teachers for their own people. This was important since few whites bothered to learn Indian languages.

The divergent approaches that whites took to Indian and African American education demonstrated broader assumptions about the two groups. Most white Americans believed that Indians were untamed and uncivilized, but not innately different from Europeans. Africans and African Americans, on the other hand, were assumed to be inferior, and most whites believed that no amount of education could change that. As U.S. frontiers expanded, white Americans considered ways to "civilize" Indians and incorporate them into the nation. But the requirements of slavery made it much more difficult for whites to imagine African Americans as anything more than lowly laborers, despite free blacks who clearly demonstrated otherwise.

Aware of the limited opportunities available in the United States, some African Americans considered the benefits of moving elsewhere. In the late 1780s, the Newport African Union Society in Rhode Island developed a plan to establish a community for American blacks in Africa. Many whites, too, viewed the settlement of blacks in Africa as the only way to solve the nation's racial dilemma.

Over the next three decades, the idea of emigration (as blacks viewed it) or colonization (as whites saw it) received widespread attention. Those who opposed slavery hoped to persuade slave owners to free or sell their human property on the condition that they be shipped

**Benjamin Banneker's** *Pennsylvania, Delaware, Maryland, and Virginia Almanac,* **1795**   Benjamin Banneker (here spelled Bannaker) was a free black from Baltimore County, Maryland. Largely self-educated, he was a talented astronomer who compiled almanacs that included annual calendars, tide charts, lunar and solar observations, and statistical charts. Almanacs were widely used by farmers, sailors, and the general public. Banneker's almanac included his portrait to highlight his achievements as a black man. Granger, NYC to Africa. Others assumed that free blacks could find opportunities in Africa that were not available to them in the United States. Still others simply wanted to rid the nation of its race problem by ridding it of blacks. In 1817 a group of southern slave owners and northern merchants formed the **American Colonization Society (ACS)** to establish colonies of freed slaves and free-born American blacks in Africa. Although some African Americans supported this scheme, northern free blacks generally opposed it, viewing colonization as an effort originating "more immediately from prejudice than philanthropy." Ultimately the plans of the ACS proved impractical. Particularly as cotton production expanded from the 1790s on, few slave owners were willing to emancipate their workers.

**A New Capital for a New Nation.** The construction of Washington City, the new capital, provided an opportunity to highlight the nation's distinctive culture and identity. But here, again, slavery emerged as a crucial part of that identity. The capital was situated along the Potomac River between Virginia and Maryland, an area where more than 300,000 enslaved workers lived. Between 1792 and 1809, hundreds of enslaved men and a few women were hired out by their owners, who were paid $5 per month for each individual's labor. Enslaved men cleared trees and stumps, built roads, dug trenches, baked bricks, and cut and laid sandstone while enslaved women cooked, did laundry, and nursed the

**The United States Capitol**    This watercolor by William Russell Birch presents a view of the Capitol in Washington, D.C., before it was burned down by the British during the War of 1812. Birch had emigrated from England in 1794 and lived in Philadelphia. As this painting suggests, neither the Capitol nor the city was as yet a vibrant center of republican achievements. Library of Congress, LC-DIG-ppmsca-22593 sick and injured. A small number performed skilled labor as carpenters or assistants to stonemasons and surveyors. Some four hundred slaves worked on the Capitol building alone, more than half the workforce.

Free blacks also participated in the development of Washington. Many worked along-side enslaved laborers, but a few held important positions. Benjamin Banneker, for example, a self-taught clock maker, astronomer, and surveyor, was hired as an assistant to the surveyor Major Andrew Ellicott. In 1791 Banneker helped to plot the 100-square-mile site on which the capital was to be built.

African Americans often worked alongside Irish immigrants, whose wages were kept in check by the availability of slave labor. Most workers, regardless of race, faced poor housing, sparse meals, malarial fevers, and limited medical care. Despite these obstacles, in less than a decade, a system of roads was laid out and cleared, the Executive Mansion was built, and the north wing of the Capitol was completed.

More prosperous immigrants and foreign professionals were also involved in creating the U.S. capital. Irish-born James Hoban designed the Executive Mansion. A French engineer developed the plan for the city's streets. A West Indian physician turned architect drew the blueprints for the Capitol building, the construction of which was directed by Englishman Benjamin Latrobe. Perhaps what was most "American" about the new capital was the diverse nationalities and races of those who designed and built it.

Washington's founders envisioned the city as a beacon to the world, proclaiming the advantages of the nation's republican principles. But its location on a slow-moving river and its clay soil left the area hot, humid, and dusty in the summer and muddy and damp in the winter and spring. When John Adams and his administration moved to Washington in June 1800, they considered themselves on the frontiers of civilization. The tree stumps that remained on the mile-long road from the Capitol to the Executive Mansion made it nearly impossible to navigate in a carriage. On rainy days, when roads proved impassable, officials walked or rode horses to work. Many early residents painted Washington in harsh tones. New Hampshire congressional representative Ebenezer Matroon wrote a friend, "If I wished to punish a culprit, I would send him to do penance in this place . . . this swamp—this lonesome dreary swamp, secluded from every delightful or pleasing thing."

Despite its critics, Washington was the seat of federal power and thus played an important role in the social and political worlds of American elites. From January through March, the height of the social season, the wives of congressmen, judges, and other officials created a lively schedule of teas, parties, and balls in the capital city. When Thomas Jefferson became president, he opened the White House to visitors on a regular basis. Yet for all his republican principles, Jefferson moved into the Executive Mansion with a retinue of slaves.

In decades to come, Washington City would become Washington, D.C., a city with broad boulevards decorated with beautiful monuments to the American political experiment. And the Executive Mansion would become the White House, a proud symbol of republican government. Yet Washington was always characterized by wide disparities in wealth, status, and power, which were especially visible when slaves labored in the Executive Mansion's kitchen, laundry, and yard. President Jefferson's efforts to incorporate new territories into the United States only exacerbated these divisions by providing more economic opportunities for planters, investors, and white farmers while ensuring the expansion of slavery and the decimation of American Indians.

## REVIEW & RELATE

- How did developments in education, literature, and the arts contribute to the emergence of a distinctly American identity?

- How did blacks and American Indians both contribute to and challenge the predominantly white view of American identity?

# Extending Federal Power

Thomas Jefferson, like other Democratic-Republicans, envisioned the United States as a republic composed of small, independent farmers who had little need and less desire for expansive federal power. Despite Jefferson's early efforts to impose this vision on the government, developments in international affairs soon converged with Supreme Court rulings to expand federal power. But Jefferson, too, contributed to this expansion. Imagining the nation's extensive frontiers as a boon to its development, he purchased the Louisiana Territory from France in 1803. The purchase and development of this vast territory increased federal authority. It also raised new questions about the place of Indians and African Americans in a republican society.

**A New Administration Faces Challenges.** In 1801 Democratic-Republicans worked quickly to implement their vision of limited federal power. Holding the majority in Congress, they repealed the whiskey tax and let the Alien and Sedition Acts expire. Jefferson significantly reduced government expenditures, and immediately set about slashing the national debt, cutting it nearly in half by the end of his second term. Democratic-Republicans also worked to curb the powers granted to the Bank of the United States and the federal court system.

Soon, however, international upheavals forced Jefferson to make fuller use of his presidential powers. The U.S. government had paid tribute to the Barbary States of North Africa during the 1790s to gain protection for American merchant ships. The new president opposed this practice and in 1801 refused to continue the payments. The Barbary pirates quickly resumed their attacks, and Jefferson was forced to send the U.S. Navy and Marine Corps to retaliate. Although a combined American and Arab force did not achieve their objective of capturing Tripoli, the Ottoman viceroy agreed to negotiate a new agreement with the United States. Seeking to avoid all-out war, Congress accepted a treaty with the Barbary States that reduced the tribute payment.

Jefferson had also followed the developing crisis in the West Indies during the 1790s. In 1791 slaves on the sugar-rich island of Saint Domingue launched a revolt against French rule. The **Haitian Revolution** escalated into a complicated conflict in which free people of color, white slave owners, and slaves formed competing alliances with British and Spanish forces as well as with leaders of the French Revolution. Finally, in December 1799, Toussaint L'Ouverture, a military leader and former slave, claimed the presidency of the new Republic of Haiti. But Napoleon Bonaparte seized power in France that same year and sent thousands of troops to reclaim the island. Toussaint was shipped off to France, where he died in prison, and many Haitians fled to the United States, but other Haitian rebels continued the fight.

**Explore ▶**

See Documents 8.2 and 8.3 for two views on the revolution in Haiti.

In the United States, reactions to the revolution were mixed, but southern whites feared that it might incite rebellions among their slaves. In 1800 Gabriel,

## COMPARATIVE ANALYSIS

# White Responses to Black Rebellion

White southerners who feared the effect of the Haitian Revolution were nonetheless shocked when Gabriel, an enslaved blacksmith, plotted a rebellion in Virginia. Upon the plot's discovery, thirty blacks were tried and convicted, and twenty-seven executed for conspiring to rebel. In the first document, President Jefferson expresses concern about slave rebellions but also about the punishment of insurgents. The second document, by Leonore Sansay, the wife of a Saint-Domingue planter, captures the situation in Haiti in 1802 as France fought to reclaim its colony. Sansay, who had earlier met Vice President Aaron Burr, writes to him about conditions on the island.

### Document 8.2

## Thomas Jefferson | Letter to U.S. Minister to Great Britain Rufus King, July 1802

The course of things in the neighboring islands of the West Indies appears to have given a considerable impulse to the minds of the slaves in different parts of the U.S. A great disposition to insurgency has manifested itself among them, which, in one instance, in the state of Virginia, broke out into actual insurrection. This was easily suppressed; but many of those concerned, (between 20 and 30, I believe) fell victims to the law. So extensive an execution could not but excite sensibility in the public mind, and beget a regret that the laws had not provided, for such cases, some alternative, combining more mildness with equal efficacy. The legislature of the state, at a subsequent meeting, took the subject into consideration, and have communicated to me . . . their wish that some place could be provided, out of the limits of the U.S., to which slaves guilty of insurgency might be transported; and they have particularly looked to Africa as offering the most desirable receptacle. We might for this purpose, enter into negotiations with the natives, on some part of the coast, to obtain a settlement and, by establishing an African company, combine with it commercial operations, which might not only reimburse expenses but procure profit also.

Source: Paul Leicester Ford, ed., *The Writings of Thomas Jefferson* (New York, 1896), 8:161–64.

an enslaved blacksmith in Richmond, Virginia, plotted such a rebellion. Inspired by both the American and Haitian revolutions, supporters rallied around the demand for "Death or Liberty." Gabriel's plan failed when informants betrayed him to authorities. Nonetheless, news of the plot traveled across the South and terrified white residents. Their anxieties were probably heightened when in November 1803, prolonged fighting, yellow fever, and the loss of sixty thousand soldiers forced Napoleon to admit defeat in Haiti. Haiti became the first independent black-led nation in the Americas.

**Acquiring the Louisiana Territory.** In France's defeat Jefferson saw an opportunity to gain navigation rights on the Mississippi River, which the French controlled. This

## Leonora Sansay | Letter to Aaron Burr, November 1802

The so much desired general Rochambeau is at length here. His arrival was announced . . . by the firing of cannon. . . . Nothing is heard of but the public joy. He is considered as the guardian, as the saviour of the people. Every proprietor feels himself already in his habitation [plantation] and I have even heard some of them disputing about the quality of the coffee they expect soon to gather. . . .

The arrival of General Rochambeau seems to have spread terror among the negroes[.] I wish they were reduced to order so that I might see the so much vaunted habitations where I should repose beneath the shade of orange groves, walk on carpets of rose leaves and Frenchipone; be fanned to sleep by silent slaves. . . .

What a delightful existence! . . .

But the moment of enjoying these pleasures is, I fear, far distant. The negroes have felt during ten years the blessing of liberty, for a blessing it certainly is, however acquired, and then will not easily be deprived of it. They have fought and vanquished French troops, and their strength has increased from a knowledge of the weakness of their opposer, and the climate itself combats for them. . . .

Every evening several old Creoles . . . assemble at our house, and talk of their affairs. One of them . . . now lives in a miserable hut. . . . Yet he still hopes for better days, in which hope they all join him.

Source: Mary Hassal [Leonora Sansay], *Secret History of the Horrors of St. Domingo, in a Series of Letters Written by a Lady at Cape François to Colonel Burr* (Philadelphia: Bradford & Inskelp, 1808), 430–32.

### Interpret the Evidence

1. How does Thomas Jefferson view the influence of West Indies rebellions on U.S. slaves, and why is he reluctant to respond to conspiracies by executing large numbers of insurgents?
2. How would you compare Leonora Sansay's response to black rebellion in Saint-Domingue/Haiti with Jefferson's response to conspiracies in Virginia? What accounts for the similarities and differences?

### Put It in Context

How might reports of the Haitian Revolution and the Virginia rebellion have contributed to debates over the future of slavery in the early years of the United States?

was a matter of crucial concern to Americans living west of the Appalachian Mountains. Jefferson sent James Monroe to France to offer Napoleon $2 million to ensure Americans the right of navigation and deposit (i.e., offloading cargo from ships) on the Mississippi. To Jefferson's surprise, Napoleon offered instead to sell the entire Louisiana Territory for $15 million.

The president agonized over the constitutionality of this **Louisiana Purchase**. Since the Constitution contained no provisions for buying land from foreign nations, a strict interpretation would prohibit the purchase. In the end, though, the opportunity proved too tempting, and the president finally agreed to buy the Louisiana Territory. Jefferson justified his decision by arguing that the territory would allow for the removal of more Indians from east of the Mississippi River, end European influence in the region, and expand U.S. trade networks. Opponents viewed the purchase as benefiting mainly agrarian interests and suspected Jefferson of trying to offset Federalist power in the Northeast. Neither party seemed especially concerned about the French, Spanish, or native peoples living in the region. They came under U.S. control when the Senate approved the purchase in October 1803. And the acquisition proved popular among ordinary Americans, most of whom focused on the opportunities it offered rather than the expansion of federal power it ensured.

At Jefferson's request, Congress had already appropriated funds for an expedition known as the **Corps of Discovery** to explore territory along the Missouri River. That expedition could now explore much of the Louisiana Territory. The president's personal secretary, Meriwether Lewis, headed the venture and invited fellow Virginian William Clark to serve as co-captain. The two set off with about forty-five men on May 14, 1804. For two years, they traveled thousands of miles up the Missouri River, through the northern plains, over the Rocky Mountains, and beyond the Louisiana Territory to the Pacific coast. Sacagawea and her husband joined them in April 1805 as they headed into the Rocky Mountains. Throughout the expedition, members meticulously recorded observations about local plants and animals as well as Indian residents, providing valuable evidence for young scientists like Parker Cleaveland and fascinating information for ordinary Americans. **See Document Project 8: The Corps of Discovery: Paeans to Peace and Instruments of War, page 270.**

Sacagawea was the only Indian to travel as a permanent member of the expedition, but many other native women and men assisted the Corps when it journeyed near their villages. They provided food and lodging for the Corps, hauled baggage up steep mountain trails, and traded food, horses, and other items. The one African American on the expedition, a slave named York, also helped negotiate trade with local Indians. York, who realized his value as a trader, hunter, and scout, asked Clark for his freedom when the expedition ended in 1806. York did eventually become a free man, but it is not clear whether it was by Clark's choice or York's escape.

Other expeditions followed Lewis and Clark's venture. In 1806 Lieutenant Zebulon Pike led a group to explore the southern portion of the Louisiana Territory (Map 8.1). After traveling from St. Louis to the Rocky Mountains, the expedition entered Mexican territory. In early 1807, Pike and his men were captured by Mexican forces. They were returned to the United States at the Louisiana border that July. Pike had learned a great deal about lands that would eventually become part of the United States and about Mexican desires to overthrow Spanish rule, information that proved valuable over the next two decades.

Early in this series of expeditions, in November 1804, Jefferson easily won reelection as president. His popularity among farmers, already high, increased when Congress reduced the minimum allotment for federal land sales from 320 to 160 acres. This act allowed more farmers to purchase land on their own rather than via speculators. Yet by the time of Jefferson's second inauguration in March 1805, the president's vision of limiting federal power had been shattered by his own actions and those of the Supreme Court.

### The Supreme Court Extends Its Reach.
In 1801, just before the Federalist-dominated Congress turned over power to the Democratic-Republicans, it passed a new **Judiciary Act**. The act created six additional circuit courts and sixteen new judgeships,

**MAP 8.1    Lewis and Clark and Zebulon Pike Expeditions, 1804–1807**

The expeditions led by Meriwether Lewis, William Clark, and Zebulon Pike illustrate the vast regions explored in just four years after the U.S. purchase of the Louisiana Territory. Journeying through and beyond the borders of that territory, the explorers gathered information about Indian nations, plants, animals, and the natural terrain even as Comanche and Shoshone nations, with access to horses, transformed the region.

which President Adams filled with Federalist "midnight appointments" before he left office. Jefferson accused the Federalists of having "retired into the judiciary" and worried that "from that battery all the works of Republicanism are to be beaten down and destroyed." Meanwhile John Marshall, chief justice of the United States (1801–1835), insisted that the powers of the Supreme Court must be equal to and balance those of the executive and legislative branches.

One of the first cases to test the Court's authority involved a dispute over President Adams's midnight appointments. Jefferson's secretary of state, James Madison, refused to deliver the appointment papers to several of the appointees, including William Marbury. Marbury and three others sued Madison to receive their commissions. In ***Marbury v. Madison*** (1803), the Supreme Court ruled that it was not empowered to force the executive branch to give Marbury his commission. But in his decision, Chief Justice Marshall declared that the Supreme Court did have the duty "to say what the law is." He thus asserted a fundamental constitutional power: that the Supreme Court had the authority to decide which federal laws were constitutional. The following year, the Court also claimed the right to rule on the constitutionality of state laws. In doing so, the Court rejected Democratic-Republicans' claim that state legislatures had the power to repudiate federal law.

Over the next dozen years, the Supreme Court continued to assert Federalist principles. In 1810 it insisted that it was the proper and sole arena for determining matters of constitutional interpretation. Then in 1819, the highest court reinforced its loose interpretation of the Constitution's implied powers clause in **McCulloch v. Maryland.** This clause gave the federal government the right to "make all laws which shall be necessary and proper" for carrying out the explicit powers granted to it by the Constitution. Despite Democratic-Republicans' earlier opposition to a national bank, Congress chartered the Second Bank of the United States in 1816, and its branch banks issued notes that circulated widely in local communities. Legislators in Maryland, believing that branch banks had gained excessive power, approved a tax on their operations. Marshall's Court ruled that the establishment of the bank was "necessary and proper" for the functioning of the national government and rejected Maryland's right to tax the branch bank, claiming that "the power to tax involves the power to destroy."

By 1820 the Supreme Court, under the forceful direction of John Marshall, had established the power of judicial review—the authority of the nation's highest court to rule on cases involving states as well as the nation. From the Court's perspective, the judiciary was as important an institution in framing and preserving a national agenda as Congress or the president.

**Democratic-Republicans Expand Federal Powers.** Although Democratic-Republicans generally opposed Marshall's rulings, they, too, continued to expand federal power. Once again, international developments drove the Jefferson administration's political agenda. By 1805 the security of the United States was threatened by continued conflicts between France and Great Britain. Both sought alliances with the young nation, and both ignored U.S. claims of neutrality. Indeed, each nation sought to punish Americans for trading with the other. Britain's Royal Navy began stopping American ships carrying sugar and molasses from the French West Indies and, between 1802 and 1811, impressed more than eight thousand sailors from such ships, including many American citizens. France claimed a similar right to stop U.S. ships that continued to trade with Great Britain.

Unable to convince foreign powers to recognize U.S. neutrality, Jefferson and Madison pushed for congressional passage of an embargo that they hoped would, like colonial boycotts, force Great Britain's hand. In 1807 Congress passed the **Embargo Act,** which prohibited U.S. ships from leaving their home ports until Britain and France repealed their restrictions on American trade. Although the act kept the United States out of war, it had a devastating impact on national commerce.

New England merchants immediately voiced their outrage, and some began sending goods to Europe via Canada. In response, Congress passed the Force Act, granting extraordinary powers to customs officials to end such smuggling. The economic pain caused by the rapid decline in trade spread well beyond the merchant class. Parker Cleaveland was forced to sell his home to the Bowdoin trustees and become their tenant. Farmers and urban workers as well as southern planters suffered the embargo's effects more directly.

**Opposition to the Embargo Act**    Although Congress repealed the Embargo Act in 1809, lawmakers still barred the United States from trading with Great Britain and France, both of which attacked American shipping in violation of U.S. neutrality. This political cartoon by Alexander Anderson criticizes the embargo, which proved costly to merchants, sailors, and dockworkers. Here a merchant carrying a barrel of goods curses the snapping turtle "Ograbme," which is *embargo* spelled backward. Granger, NYC

Exports nearly stopped, and sailors and dockworkers faced escalating unemployment. With the recession deepening, American concerns about the expansion of federal power reemerged. Congress and the president had not simply regulated international trade; they had brought it to a halt.

Still, despite the failure of the Embargo Act, many Americans viewed Jefferson favorably. He had devoted his adult life to the creation of the United States. He had purchased the Louisiana Territory, opening up vast lands to American exploration and development. This geographical boon encouraged inventors and artisans to pursue ideas that would help the early republic take full advantage of its resources and recover from its current economic plight. Some must have wondered, however, how a Democratic-Republican president had so significantly expanded the power of the federal government.

## REVIEW & RELATE

How did the Federalist-dominated courts and the Democratic-Republican president and Congress each contribute to the expansion of the federal government?

How did the purchase of the Louisiana Territory from France and international conflicts with France and Britain shape domestic issues in the late eighteenth and early nineteenth centuries?

# Remaking America's Economic Character

As the United States expanded geographically, technological ingenuity became a highly valued commodity. The spread of U.S. settlements into new territories necessitated improved forms of transportation and communication and increased demands for muskets and other weapons to protect the nation's frontier. The growing population also fueled improvements in agriculture and manufacturing to meet demands for clothing, food, and farm equipment. Continued conflicts with Great Britain and France also highlighted the need to develop the nation's natural resources and technological capabilities. Yet even though American ingenuity was widely praised, the daily lives of most Americans changed slowly. And for some, especially enslaved women and men, technological advances only added to their burdens.

**The U.S. Population Grows and Migrates.** Although Democratic-Republicans initially hoped to limit the powers of the national government, the rapid growth of the United States pulled in the opposite direction. An increased population, combined with the exhaustion of farmland along the eastern seaboard, fueled migration to the West as well as the growth of cities. These developments heightened conflicts with Indians and over slavery, but they also encouraged innovations in transportation and communication and improvements in agriculture and manufacturing.

As white Americans encroached more deeply on lands long settled by native peoples, Indian tribes were forced ever westward. As early as 1800, groups like the Shoshone, who originally inhabited the Great Plains, had been forced into the Rocky Mountains by Indians moving into the plains from the Mississippi and Ohio valleys (Map 8.2). Sacagawea must have realized that the expedition she accompanied would only increase pressure on the Shoshone and other nations as white migration escalated.

Although the vast majority of Americans continued to live in rural areas, a growing number moved to cities as eastern farmland lost its fertility and young people sought job opportunities in manufacturing, skilled trades, and service work. Cities were defined at the time as places with 8,000 or more inhabitants, but New York City and Philadelphia both counted more than 100,000 residents by 1810. In New York, immigrants, most of them Irish, made up about 10 percent of the population in 1820 and twice that percentage five years later. At the same time, the number of African Americans in New York City increased to more than 10,000. Cities began to emerge along the nation's frontier as well. After the Louisiana Purchase, New Orleans became a key commercial center while western migration fueled cities like Cincinnati. Even smaller frontier towns, like Rock Island, Illinois, served important functions for migrants traveling west. Trading posts appeared across the Mississippi valley, which eased the migration of thousands headed farther west. They served as sites of exchange between Indians and white Americans and created the foundations for later cities (Table 8.1).

Most Americans who headed west hoped to benefit from the increasingly liberal terms for land offered by the federal government. Yeomen farmers sought sufficient acreage to feed their families and grow some crops for sale. They were eager to settle in western sections of the original thirteen states, in the Ohio River valley, or in newly opened territories along the Missouri and Kansas Rivers. In the South, small farmers had to compete with slave-owning planters who headed west in the early nineteenth century. Migrants to the Mississippi valley also had to contend with a sizable population of Spanish and French residents, as well as Chickasaw and Creek Indians in the South and Shawnee, Chippewa, Sauk, and Fox communities farther north.

The development of roads and turnpikes hastened the movement of people and the transportation of goods. Frontier farmers wanted to get their produce to eastern markets quickly and cheaply. Before completion of the Lancaster Turnpike in Pennsylvania, it cost as much to carry wheat overland the sixty-two miles to Philadelphia as it did to ship it by sea from Philadelphia to London. Those who lived farther west faced even greater challenges. With the admission of Kentucky (1792), Tennessee (1796), and Ohio (1803) to the Union,

**MAP 8.2   Indian Land Cessions, 1790–1820**

With the ratification of the Constitution, the federal government gained greater control over Indian relations, including land cessions. At the same time, large numbers of white settlers poured into regions west of the Appalachian Mountains. The U.S. government gained most Indian land by purchase or treaty, but these agreements were often the consequence of military victories by the U.S. Army.

**TABLE 8.1    Prices at George Davenport's Trading Post, Rock Island, Illinois, c. 1820**

| Item | Price | Item | Price |
|------|-------|------|-------|
| Ax | $6.00 | Large copper kettle | $30.00 |
| Beaver trap | $8.00 | Lead | $0.20 per pound |
| Black silk handkerchief | $2.00 | Lead shot for guns | $1.00 per 5 pounds |
| Breechcloth | $3.00 | Medium copper kettle | $10.00 |
| Bridles | $2.00–$10.00 | Muskrat spear | $2.00 |
| Chain for staking down traps | $0.75 per 6 feet | Muskrat trap | $5.00 |
| Combs | $1.00 per pair | Muslin or calico shirt | $3.00 |
| File (for sharpening axes) | $2.00 | Ordinary butcher knife | $0.50 |
| Flannel | $1.00 per yard | Sheet iron kettle | $10.00 |
| Flannel mantle | $3.00 | Small copper kettle | $3.00 |
| Gunflints | $1.00 per 15 | Spurs | $6.00 per pair |
| Hand-size mirrors | $0.25 | Tin kettle | $14.00 |
| Heavy wool cloth | $10.00 per yard | Tomahawk | $1.50 |
| Hoe | $2.00 | Trade gun | $20.00–$25.00 |
| Horn of gunpowder | $1.50 | Wool blanket | $4.00 |
| Horses | $35.00–$50.00 | Wool mantle (short cloak or shawl) | $4.00 |

Source: Will Leinicke, Marion Lardner, and Ferrel Anderson, *Two Nations, One Land* (Rock Island, IL: Citizens to Preserve Black Hawk Park, 1981).

demands for congressional support for building transportation routes grew louder. By 1819 five more states had been admitted along the Mississippi River, from Louisiana to Illinois.

During Jefferson's administration, secretary of the treasury Albert Gallatin urged Congress to fund roads and canals to enhance the economic development of the nation. He advocated a "great turnpike road" along the Atlantic seaboard from Maine to Georgia as well as roads to connect the four main rivers that flowed from the Appalachians to the Atlantic Ocean. Although traditionally such projects were funded by the states, in 1815 Congress approved funds for a **National Road** from western Maryland through southwestern Pennsylvania to Wheeling, West Virginia. This so-called Cumberland Road was completed in 1818 and later extended into Ohio and Illinois.

Carrying people and goods by water was even faster and cheaper than transporting them over land, but rivers ran mainly north and south. In addition, although loads could be delivered quickly downstream, the return voyage was long and slow. While politicians advocated the construction of canals along east-west routes to link river systems, inventors and mechanics focused on building boats powered by steam to overcome the problems of sending goods upriver.

In 1804 Oliver Evans, a machinist in Philadelphia, invented a high-pressure steam engine attached to a dredge that cleaned the silt around the docks in Philadelphia harbor. He had insufficient funds, however, to pursue work on a steam-powered boat. Robert Fulton, a New Yorker, improved on Evans's efforts, using the low-pressure steam engine developed in England. In 1807 Fulton launched the first successful steamboat, the *Clermont*, which traveled up the Hudson River from New York City to Albany in only thirty-two hours. The powerful Mississippi River proved a greater challenge, but by combining Evans's high-pressure steam engine with a flat-bottom hull that avoided the river's sandbars, mechanics who worked along the frontier improved Fulton's design and launched the steamboat era in the West.

**Technology Reshapes Agriculture and Industry.** Advances in agricultural and industrial technology paralleled the development of roads and steamboats. Here, too, a single invention spurred others, inducing a **multiplier effect** that inspired additional dramatic changes. Two inventions—the cotton gin and the spinning machine—were especially notable in transforming southern agriculture and northern industry, transformations that were deeply intertwined.

American developments were also closely tied to the earlier rise of industry in Great Britain. By the 1770s, British manufacturers had built spinning mills in which steampowered machines spun raw cotton into yarn. Eager to maintain their monopoly on industrial technology, the British made it illegal for engineers to emigrate. They could not stop

**Samuel Slater's Mill, c. 1790**   This eighteenth-century painting by an unknown American artist depicts the first cotton mill built in the United States. Constructed by Samuel Slater on the Blackstone River in Pawtucket, Rhode Island, the mill stands next to a waterfall, which supplies the power to run the machinery. While portraying a major industrial innovation, the artist highlights its pastoral setting. Smithsonian Institution, Washington DC, USA/Bridgeman Images everyone who worked in a cotton mill, however, from leaving. At age fourteen, Samuel Slater was hired as an apprentice in an English mill that used a yarn-spinning machine designed by Richard Arkwright. Slater was promoted to supervisor of the factory, but at age twenty-one he sought greater opportunities in America. While working in New York City, he learned that Moses Brown, a wealthy Rhode Island merchant, was eager to develop a machine like Arkwright's. Funded by Rhode Island investors and assisted by local craftsmen, Slater designed and built a spinning mill in Pawtucket.

The mill opened in December 1790 and began producing yarn, which was then woven into cloth in private shops and homes. By 1815 a series of cotton mills dotted the Pawtucket River. These factories offered workers, most of whom were the wives and children of farmers, a steady income, and they ensured employment for weavers in the countryside. They also increased the demand for cotton in New England just as British manufacturers sought new sources of the crop as well.

**Explore ▶**

See Document 8.4 for a description of mills in Worcester, Massachusetts.

Ensuring a steady supply of cotton required another technological innovation, this one created by Eli Whitney. After graduating from Yale, Whitney agreed to serve as a private tutor for a planter family in South Carolina. On the ship carrying him south, Whitney met the widow Catherine Greene, who invited him to stay at her Mulberry Plantation near Savannah, Georgia. There local planters complained to him about the difficulty of making a profit on cotton. Long-staple cotton, grown in the Sea Islands, yielded enormous profits, but the soil in most of the South could sustain only the short-staple variety, which required hours of intensive labor to separate its sticky green seeds from the cotton fiber.

In 1793, in as little as ten days, Eli Whitney built a machine that could speed the process of deseeding short-staple cotton. Using mesh screens, rollers, and wire brushes, Whitney's **cotton gin** could clean as much cotton fiber in one hour as several workers could

**The Cotton Gin, 1793**   This colored lithograph by an anonymous American artist shows Eli Whitney's cotton gin at the center of complex transactions. Enslaved women and men haul and gin cotton. Meanwhile the planter appears to be bargaining with a cotton factor, or agent, who likely wants to purchase his crop for a northern manufacturer. Private Collection/Peter Newark American Pictures/Bridgeman Images clean in a day. Recognizing the gin's value, Whitney received a U.S. patent, but because the machine was easy to duplicate, he never profited from his invention.

Fortunately, Whitney had other ideas that proved more profitable. In June 1798, amid U.S. fears of a war with France, the U.S. government granted him an extraordinary contract to produce 4,000 rifles in eighteen months. Adapting the plan of Honoré Blanc, a French mechanic who devised a musket with interchangeable parts, Whitney demonstrated the potential for using machines to produce various parts of a musket, which could then be assembled in mass quantities. With Jefferson's enthusiastic support, the federal government extended Whitney's contract, and by 1809 his New Haven factory was turning

## SOLO ANALYSIS

## Timothy Dwight | Visit to Worcester (Massachusetts) Mills, 1821

American industry began in earnest in New England, and mills there garnered great attention from interested observers at home and abroad. In 1821 Timothy Dwight, the president of Yale College, published his impression of various New England towns in his *Travels*, including the bustling commercial center of Worcester, Massachusetts. After describing the town and the great variety of mills located along the Blackstone River, he notes the ubiquity of such mills throughout New England.

### Document 8.4

Few towns in New-England exhibit so uniform an appearance of neatness and taste or contain so great a proportion of good buildings, and so small a proportion of those which are indifferent, as Worcester. There is probably more wealth in it also than in any other, which does not exceed it in dimensions and number of inhabitants. Its trade, considering its inland situation, is believed to be extensive and profitable. . . .

There are in Worcester four grist-mills, four saw-mills, two fulling-mills, and a large paper-mill. The proprietors of the fulling-mills carry on the Clothiers' business to a great extent; and with skill supposed not to be excelled in the State. Scarlet and blue have for some time been dyed here in a superior manner.

On the subject of *mills* I wish you to observe, once for all, that I shall rarely mention them. There is scarcely a township in New-England which has not a complete set of grist-mills and saw-mills. . . . There is, probably, no country in the world where mill-streams are so numerously and universally dispersed, or grist-mills and saw-mills so universally erected as in New-England. Conveniences of this kind may be said, almost if not quite literally, to be furnished in abundance to every Parish in the Country. To reiterate this fact would be to take very effectual means for wearing out your patience.

Source: Timothy Dwight, *Travels; in New-England and New-York* (New Haven: Timothy Dwight, 1821), 366–67.

### Interpret the Evidence

1. How does Dwight characterize Worcester? What role do the mills play in his assessment?
2. Why does Dwight say he is not going to discuss mills elsewhere in his book?

### Put It in Context

What does Dwight's report reveal about the industrial innovations occurring in the northeastern United States in the early nineteenth century?

out 7,500 guns annually. Whitney's factory became a model for the **American system of manufacturing**, in which water-powered machinery and the division of production into several small tasks allowed less skilled workers to produce mass quantities of a particular item. Moreover, the factories developed by Whitney and Slater became training grounds for younger mechanics and inventors who devised improvements in machinery or set out to solve new technological puzzles. Their efforts also transformed the lives of generations of workers—enslaved and free—who planted and picked the cotton, spun the yarn, wove the cloth, and sewed the clothes that cotton gins and spinning mills made possible.

### Transforming Household Production.

Slater and Whitney were among the most influential American inventors, but both required the assistance and collaboration of other inventors, machinists, and artisans to implement their ideas. The achievement of these enterprising individuals was seen by many Americans as part of a larger spirit of inventiveness and technological ingenuity that characterized U.S. identity. Although many Americans built on foreign ideas and models, a cascade of inventions did appear in the United States between 1790 and 1820.

Cotton gins and steam engines, steamboats and interchangeable parts, gristmills and spinning mills—each of these items and processes was improved over time and led to myriad other inventions. For instance, in 1811 Francis Cabot invented a power loom for weaving, a necessary step once spinning mills began producing more yarn than hand weavers could handle.

Despite these rapid technological advances, the changes that occurred in the early nineteenth century were more evolutionary than revolutionary. Most political leaders and social commentators viewed gradual improvement as a blessing. For many Americans, the ideal situation consisted of either small mills scattered through the countryside or household enterprises that could supply neighbors with finer cloth, wool cards, or other items that improved home production.

The importance of domestic manufacturing increased after passage of the Embargo Act as imports of cloth and other items fell dramatically. Small factories, like those along the Pawtucket River, increased their output, and so did ordinary housewives. Blacksmiths, carpenters, and wheelwrights busily repaired and improved the spindles, looms, and other equipment that allowed family members to produce more and better cloth from wool, flax, and cotton. New ideas about companionate marriage, which emphasized mutual obligations, may have encouraged husbands and wives to work more closely in these domestic enterprises. While husbands generally carried out the heavier or more skilled parts of home manufacturing, like weaving, wives spun yarn and sewed together sections of cloth into finished goods.

At the same time, daughters, neighbors, and servants remained critical to the production of household items. In early nineteenth-century Hallowell, Maine, Martha Ballard labored alongside her daughters and a niece, producing cloth and food for domestic consumption, while she supplemented her husband's income as a surveyor by working as a midwife. Yet older forms of mutuality also continued, with neighbors sharing tools and equipment and those with specialized skills assisting neighbors in exchange for items they needed. Perhaps young couples imagined themselves embarking on more egalitarian marriages than those of their parents, but most still needed wider networks of support.

In wealthy households north and south, servants and slaves took on a greater share of domestic labor in the late eighteenth and early nineteenth centuries. Most female servants in the North were young and unmarried. Some arrived with children in tow or became pregnant while on the job, a mark of the rising rate of out-of-wedlock births following the Revolution. Planters' wives in the South had fewer worries in this regard because if household slaves became pregnant, their children added to the owner's labor supply. Moreover, on larger plantations, owners increasingly assigned a few enslaved women to spin, cook, wash clothes, make candles, and wait on table. Plantation mistresses might also hire the wives of small farmers and landless laborers to spin cotton into yarn, weave yarn into cloth, and sew clothing for slaves and children. While mistresses in both regions still engaged in household production, they expanded their roles as domestic managers.

However, most Americans at the turn of the nineteenth century continued to live on family farms, to produce or trade locally to meet their needs, and to use techniques handed down for generations. Yet by 1820, their lives, like those of wealthier Americans, were transformed by the expanding market economy. More and more families sewed clothes with machine-spun thread made from cotton ginned in the American South, worked their fields with newly invented cast-iron plows, and varied their diet by adding items shipped from other regions by steamboat.

**Technology, Cotton, and Slaves.** Some of the most dramatic technological changes occurred in agriculture, and none was more significant than the cotton gin, which led to the vast expansion of agricultural production and slavery in the South. This in turn fueled regional specialization, ensuring that residents in one area of the nation—the North, South, or West—depended on those in other areas. Southern planters relied on a growing demand for cotton from northern merchants and manufacturers. At the same time, planters, merchants, manufacturers, and factory workers became more dependent on western farmers to produce grain and livestock to feed the nation.

As cotton gins spread across the South, cotton and slavery expanded into the interior of many southern states as well as into the lower Mississippi valley. While rice and sugar were also produced in the South, cotton quickly became the most important crop. In 1790 southern farms and plantations produced about 3,000 bales of cotton, each weighing about 300 pounds. By 1820, with the aid of the cotton gin, the South produced more than 330,000 bales annually (Table 8.2). For southern blacks, increased production meant increased burdens. Because seeds could be separated from raw cotton with much greater efficiency, farmers could plant vastly larger quantities of the crop. Although family members, neighbors, and hired hands performed this work on small farms with only a few or no slaves, wealthy planters, with perhaps a dozen slaves, took advantage of rising cotton prices in the early eighteenth century to purchase more slaves.

The dramatic increase in the amount of cotton planted and harvested each year was paralleled by a jump in the size of the slave population. Thus, even as northern states began to abolish

**TABLE 8.2 Growth of Cotton Production in the United States, 1790–1830**

| Year | Production in Bales |
|------|---------------------|
| 1790 | 3,135 |
| 1795 | 16,719 |
| 1800 | 73,145 |
| 1805 | 146,290 |
| 1810 | 177,638 |
| 1815 | 208,986 |
| 1820 | 334,378 |
| 1825 | 532,915 |
| 1830 | 731,452 |

Source: Lewis Cecil Gray, *History of Agriculture in the Southern United States to 1860*, vol. 2 (Gloucester, MA: Peter Smith, 1958).

the institution, southern planters significantly increased the number of slaves they held. In 1790 there were fewer than 700,000 slaves in the United States. By 1820 there were nearly 1.5 million. Despite this population increase, growing competition for field hands drove up the price of slaves, which roughly doubled between 1795 and 1805.

Although the international slave trade was banned in the United States in 1808, some planters smuggled in women and men from Africa and the Caribbean. Most planters, however, depended on enslaved women to bear more children, increasing the size of their labor force through natural reproduction. In addition, planters in the Deep South—from Georgia and the Carolinas west to Louisiana—began buying slaves from farmers in Maryland and Virginia, where cotton and slavery were less profitable. Expanding slave markets in New Orleans and Charleston marked the continued importance of this domestic or internal slave trade as cotton moved west.

In the early nineteenth century, most white southerners believed that there was enough land to go around. And the rising price of cotton allowed small farmers to imagine they would someday be planters. Some southern Indians also placed their hopes in cotton. Cherokee and Creek Indians cultivated the crop, even purchasing black slaves to increase production. Some Indian villages now welcomed ministers to their communities, hoping that embracing white culture might allow them to retain their current lands. Yet other native residents foresaw the increased pressure for land that cotton cultivation produced and organized to defend themselves from whites' invasion. Regardless of the policies adopted by Indians, cotton and slavery expanded rapidly into Cherokee- and Creek-controlled lands in the interior of Georgia and South Carolina. And the admission of the states of Louisiana, Mississippi, and Alabama between 1812 and 1819 marked the rapid spread of southern agriculture farther west.

Enslaved men and women played critical roles in the South's geographical expansion. Without their labor, neither cotton nor sugar could have become mainstays of the South's economy. The heavy work of carving out new plantations led most planters to select young slave men and women to move west, breaking apart families in the process. Some slaves resisted their removal and, if forced to go, used their role in the labor process to limit owners' control. Slaves resisted by working slowly, breaking tools, and feigning illness or injury. Other enslaved women and men hid out temporarily as a respite from brutal work regimes or harsh punishments. Still others ran to areas controlled by Indians, hoping for better treatment, or to regions where slavery was no longer legal.

Yet given the power and resources wielded by whites, most slaves had to find ways to improve their lives within the system of bondage. The end of the international slave trade helped blacks in this regard since planters had to depend more on natural reproduction to increase their labor supply. To ensure that slaves lived longer and healthier lives, planters were forced to provide better food, shelter, and clothing. Some slaves gained leverage to fish, hunt, or maintain small gardens to improve their diet. With the birth of more children, southern blacks also developed more extensive kinship networks, which often allowed other family members to care for children if their parents were compelled to move west. Enslavement was still brutal, but slaves made small gains that improved their chances of survival.

Southern slaves also established their own religious ceremonies, often held in the woods or swamps at night. African Americans were swept up as well in the religious revivals that burned across the southern frontier beginning in the 1790s. Itinerant preachers held camp meetings that tapped into deep emotional wells of spirituality. Baptist and Methodist clergy drew free and enslaved blacks as well as white frontier families to their gatherings and encouraged physical displays of spiritual rebirth, offering poor blacks and whites release from the oppressive burdens of daily life through dancing, shaking, and shouting.

Evangelical religion, combined with revolutionary ideals promoted in the United States and Haiti, proved a potent mix, and planters rarely lost sight of the potential dangers this posed to the system of bondage. Outright rebellions occurred only rarely, yet victory in Haiti and Gabriel's conspiracy in Virginia reminded slaves and owners alike that uprisings were possible. Clearly, the power of new American identities could not be separated from the dangers embedded in the nation's oppressive racial history.

## REVIEW & RELATE

- How did new inventions and infrastructure improvements contribute to the development of the American economy?

- Why did slavery expand and become more deeply entrenched in southern society in the early nineteenth century? What fears did this reinforce?

# Conclusion: New Identities and New Challenges

The geographical and economic expansion that marked the period from 1790 to 1820 inspired scientific and technological advances as well as literary and artistic tributes to a distinctly American identity. For young ambitious men like Parker Cleaveland, Eli Whitney, Washington Irving, and Meriwether Lewis, the opportunities that opened in education, science, literature, and exploration offered possibilities for fame and financial success. While Whitney, Irving, and Lewis traveled widely, Cleaveland remained a professor of mathematics, mineralogy, and chemistry at Bowdoin, dying in Brunswick, Maine, in 1858.

Lewis's efforts to open up the Louisiana Territory transformed the lives of many Americans. Along with the construction of roads, the invention of steamboats, and the introduction of iron plows, his Corps of Discovery opened up new lands for farming and also fueled the rise of western cities. Many white families sought fertile land, abundant wildlife, or opportunities for trade on the frontier. Yet these families often had to purchase land from speculators or compete with wealthy planters. And those who carved out farms might face Indians angered by the constant encroachment of white Americans on their lands.

New opportunities also appeared in eastern towns and cities as investors, inventors, and skilled artisans established factories and improved transportation. White women of middling or elite status could attend female academies, enter marriages based on ideals of companionship and mutual responsibilities, purchase rather than make cotton thread and cloth, and retain servants to perform the heaviest work. Yet these changes occurred gradually and unevenly. And while poorer white women might more easily find jobs in cotton mills or as servants, the pay was low and the hours long.

Transformations in white society introduced even more difficult challenges for African Americans. Despite the introduction of gradual emancipation in the North and the end of the international slave trade, slavery continued to grow. The invention of the cotton gin ensured the expansion of cotton cultivation into new areas, and many slaves were forced to move west and leave family and friends behind. Enslaved women and men honed means of survival and resistance, but few could imagine a revolution like the one that took place in Haiti.

At the same time, all along the expanding U.S. frontier, American Indians faced continued pressure to leave their lands, embrace white culture, or both. In 1810 Sacagawea, Charbonneau, and their son Baptiste apparently traveled to St. Louis at the invitation of William Clark, who offered to pay for Baptiste's schooling. Sacagawea left Baptiste in Clark's care, and it is not clear whether she ever saw her son again. William Clark wrote "Se car ja we au Dead" on the cover of his cash book for 1825–1828, suggesting that she died during those years. By then, the Shoshone and Hidatsa were facing the onslaught of white settlement. They, along with Indians living in areas like Georgia, the Carolinas, and Tennessee, continued to resist U.S. expansion and struggled to control the embattled frontier.

Indeed, the United States remained embattled throughout the early years of the republic. From 1790 to 1820, Great Britain, France, and the Barbary States of North Africa constantly challenged U.S. sovereignty from abroad while debates over slavery and conflicts over Indian lands multiplied at home. Moreover, as federal power expanded under Democratic-Republic rule, some Americans continued to worry about protecting the rights of states and of individuals. The American identities forged in the early republic would be continually tested as new challenges emerged and older conflicts intensified in the following decades.

## TIMELINE OF **EVENTS**

| | |
|---|---|
| **1789** | Massachusetts institutes free public elementary education |
| **1790** | Samuel Slater's spinning mill opens |
| **1790–1820** | Cotton production in the South increases from 3,000 to 330,000 bales annually |
| | U.S. slave population rises from 700,000 to 1.5 million |
| **1791–1803** | Haitian Revolution |
| **1792–1809** | New capital of Washington City constructed |
| **1793** | Eli Whitney invents cotton gin |
| **1801** | Judiciary Act |
| | U.S. forces challenge Barbary pirates |
| **1803** | Louisiana Purchase |
| | *Marbury v. Madison* |
| **1804–1806** | Corps of Discovery explores Louisiana Territory and Pacific Northwest |
| **1807** | Robert Fulton launches first successful steamboat |
| | Embargo Act |
| **1810** | Population of New York and Philadelphia each exceeds 100,000 |
| **1817** | American Colonization Society founded |
| **1819** | *McCulloch v. Maryland* |
| **1820** | Washington Irving publishes *Sketchbook* |
| **1828** | Noah Webster publishes *American Dictionary of the English Language* |

## KEY **TERMS**

American Colonization Society (ACS), *249*

Haitian Revolution, *251*

Louisiana Purchase, *253*

Corps of Discovery, *254*

Judiciary Act, *254*

*Marbury v. Madison*, *255*

*McCulloch v. Maryland*, *256*

Embargo Act, *256*

National Road, *260*

multiplier effect, *261*

cotton gin, *262*

American system of manufacturing, *264*

## REVIEW & RELATE

1. How did developments in education, literature, and the arts contribute to the emergence of a distinctly American identity?

2. How did blacks and American Indians both contribute to and challenge the predominantly white view of American identity?

3. How did the Federalist-dominated courts and the Democratic-Republican president and Congress each contribute to the expansion of the federal government?

4. How did the purchase of the Louisiana Territory from France and international conflicts with France and Britain shape domestic issues in the late eighteenth and early nineteenth centuries?

5. How did new inventions and infrastructure improvements contribute to the development of the American economy?

6. Why did slavery expand and become more deeply entrenched in southern society in the early nineteenth century? What fears did this reinforce?

# The Corps of Discovery: Paeans to Peace and Instruments of War

From 1804 to 1806, the Corps of Discovery mapped vast regions of the West, documented plants and animals, and initiated trade relations with Indian nations. When the Corps built its winter camp at Fort Mandan in October 1804, its members hoped to develop commercial relations with local Mandan, Hidatsa, and Arikara villages. Most of these tribes had been ravaged by smallpox in the early 1780s and were now subject to raids by more powerful nations in the region. Meriwether Lewis and William Clark hoped to persuade all of these nations that peaceful relations would benefit them politically and economically. To aid negotiations, the Corps offered gifts to the Indian leaders they encountered (Document 8.5). The Mandan, however, expected more gifts than the expedition could offer. Although Lewis and Clark assured Mandan leaders they would benefit from future trade with and protection from the United States, the Indians had heard such promises before and were wary of giving away vital food as winter descended (Document 8.6).

Worried about surviving the winter, Lewis and Clark finally found an unexpected item to trade with the Mandan. When their men finished building a smithy in December 1804, they discovered that Indians would exchange almost any item for metal hatchets, especially those designed for battle (Documents 8.7 and 8.8).

In April the Corps moved west into present-day Idaho and traded with Shoshone leaders for horses. The Shoshone were engaged in a long and lucrative trade in horses with the Comanche, who had split from the Shoshones, moved south, and developed ties with the Spanish. But the Shoshone had a harder time getting guns, a concern they expressed to Lewis (Document 8.9). While Lewis and Clark advocated peace among Indian nations, one of their most desired trade items was weaponry. When their explorations inspired white settlement in this vast western territory, that weaponry would become more important than ever.

## Document 8.5

### William Clark, Journal | October 12, 1804

As the Corps of Discovery traveled up the Missouri River from St. Louis, they stopped at Indian villages along the way to advocate peace; offer presents from President Jefferson; and learn about local plants, animals, and potential trade items. In his journal entry for October 12, William Clark describes a visit to a Ricara (Arikara) village near where the Corps planned to stay for the winter.

After breakfast, we went on shore to the house of the chief of the second village named Lassel, where we found his chiefs and warriors. They made us a present of about seven bushels of corn, a pair of leggings, a twist of their tobacco, and the seeds of two different species of tobacco. The chief then delivered a speech expressive of his gratitude for the presents and the good counsels which we had given him; his intention of visiting his great father [the president of the United States] but for fear of the Sioux; and requested us to take one of the Ricara chiefs up to the Mandans and negotiate a peace between the two nations. . . . After we had answered and explained the magnitude and power of the United States, the three chiefs came with us to the boat. We gave them some sugar, a little salt, and a sun-glass. Two of them left us, and the chief of the third [village] . . . accompanied us to the Mandans.

[T]he Ricaras . . . were originally colonies of Pawnees, who established themselves on the Missouri. . . . From that situation, a part of the Ricaras emigrated to the neighbourhood of the Mandans, with whom they were then in alliance. The rest of the nation continued near the Chayenne [Cheyenne] till the year 1797, in the course of which, distressed by their wars with the Sioux, they joined their countrymen near the Mandans. Soon after a new war arose between the Ricaras and the Mandans, in consequence of which the former came down the river to their present position. . . .

They [the Ricara] express a disposition to keep at peace with all nations, but they are well armed with fusils [muskets], and being much under the influence of the Sioux, who exchanged the goods which they got from the British for Ricara corn, their minds are sometimes poisoned and they cannot always be depended on.

Source: William Clark Journal, October 12, 1804, *History of the Expeditions of Captains Lewis and Clark, 1804-5-6, Reprinted from the Edition of 1814, with Introduction and Index by James K. Hosmer* (Chicago: A. C. McClurg, 1902), 1:110–11, 114.

Document 8.6

## Charles McKenzie | Narrative of a Fur Trader, November 1804

Charles McKenzie was a Scotsman working as a clerk for the Hudson Bay Company. He arrived with six traders at a Hidatsa village in November 1804. Over time, McKenzie adopted Indian dress, married an Indian woman, and became an advocate for Indian concerns. Here he recounts Lewis's frustration in his efforts to gain favor with local Indians as well as Mandan concerns about the Corps' lack of generosity.

Here we also found a party of forty Americans under the command of Captains Lewis and Clark exploring a passage by the Mississouri [Missouri] to the Pacific Ocean—they came up the River in a Boat of twenty oars accompanied by two *Peroque*s [open boats or canoes]. Their fortifications for winter Quarters were already complete—they had held a council with the Mandanes, and

distributed many presents; but most of the Chiefs did not accept any thing from them. Some time after Captain Lewis with three Interpreters paid a visit to the *Gros Ventres* [Hidatsa] Village. . . . [N]ext morning he came to the village where I was—and observed to me that he was not very graciously received at the upper Village. . . .

After haranguing the Indians and explaining to them the purport of his [Lewis's] expedition to the Westward, several of them accepted clothing—but notwithstanding they could not be reconciled to like these strangers as they called them:—"Had these Whites come amongst us, Said the Chiefs, with charitable views they would have loaded their Great Boat with necessaries [trade items]. It is true they have ammunition but they prefer throwing it away idly [shooting in the air] than sparing a shot of it to a poor Mandane." . . . "Had I these White warriors in the upper plains, said the *Gros Ventres* Chief, my young men on horseback would soon do for them, as they would do for so many wolves—for, continued he, there are only two sensible men among them—the worker of Iron, and the mender of Guns."

The American Gentlemen gave flags and medals to the Chiefs on condition that they should not go to war unless the enemy attacked them in their Villages. Yet the Chief of the wolves, whose brother had been killed in the fall previous to our arrival, went soon after with a party of fifty men to revenge his death.

Source: W. Raymond Wood and Thomas D. Thiessen, eds., *Early Fur Trade on the Northern Plains: Canadian Traders among the Mandan and Hidatsa Indians, 1738–1818* (Norman: University of Oklahoma Press, 1985), 232–33.

Document 8.7

## William Clark | Journal, November 18, 1804

By November 1804, the Corps had built and settled into Fort Mandan, at the convergence of the Missouri and Knife Rivers, for the winter. Lewis and Clark became increasingly aware that their trade with particular groups, like the Mandans, might shift the balance of power in the region. But given the extended journey ahead, they were limited in what goods they could give or trade with local Indians even as they sought to reassure them of U.S. support.

To-day we had a cold windy morning; the Black Cat [a Mandan chief] came to see us, and occupied us for a long time with questions on the usages [customs] of our country. He mentioned that a council had been held yesterday to deliberate on the state of their affairs. It seems that not long ago a party of Sioux fell in with some horses belonging to the Minnetarees and carried them off, but in their flight they were met by some Assiniboins, who killed the Sioux and kept the horses. A Frenchman, too, who had lived many years among the Mandans, was lately killed on his route to the British factory [trading post] on the Assiniboin . . . , all of which being discussed, the council decided that they would not resent the recent insults from the Assiniboins . . . until they had seen whether we had deceived them or not in our promises of furnishing them with arms and ammunition. They had been disappointed in their hopes of receiving them from Mr. Evans, and were afraid that we, too, like him, might tell them what was not true. We advised them to continue at peace, that supplies of every kind would no doubt arrive for them, but that time was necessary to organize the trade. The fact is that the Assiniboins treat the Mandans as the Sioux do the Ricaras; by their vicinity to the British they get all the supplies, which they withhold or give at pleasure to the remoter Indians; the consequence is that, however badly treated, the Mandans and Ricaras are very slow to retaliate lest they should lose their trade altogether.

Source: William Clark Journal, November 18, 1804, *History of the Expeditions of Captains Lewis and Clark, 1804-5-6, Reprinted from the Edition of 1814, with Introduction and Index by James K. Hosmer* (Chicago: A. C. McClurg, 1902), 1:136–37.

Document 8.8

## William Clark | Journal, January 28, 1805, and Meriwether Lewis, Journal, February 1, 1805

By early 1805 it was clear to Lewis and Clark that metal goods, especially axes or hatchets, were the most valuable means of obtaining the corn and other items they needed from the Mandans and neighboring Indians. These two short entries, by Clark and then Lewis, describe the value of the trade in hatchets to the Corps and their continued commitment to peace among Indian nations.

American Philosophical Society

28th January

Attempt to cut through the ice to get our Boat and Canoes out without success. Several Indians here wishing to get war hatchets made [image of one drawn here]. The man sick yesterday is getting well Mr. Jessome [Jessaume], our interpreter was taken very unwell this evening. Warm day.

1st February

A cold, windy day. . . . One of the Minnetaree chiefs . . . came to see us and procure a war hatchet; he also requested that we would suffer him to go to war against the Sioux and Ricaras, who had killed a Mandan some time ago; this we refused for reasons which we explained to him. He acknowledged that we were right, and promised to open his ears to our counsel.

Source: William Clark Journal, January 28, 1805, Codex C: 158 American Philosophical Society, Courtesy of the American Philosophical Society Library; and Meriwether Lewis Journal, February 1, 1805, *History of the Expeditions of Captains Lewis and Clark, 1804-5-6, Reprinted from the Edition of 1814, with Introduction and Index by James K. Hosmer* (Chicago: A. C. McClurg, 1902), 1:168.

---

**Document 8.9**

## Meriwether Lewis | Journal, August 20, 1805

The Corps was eager to encounter the Shoshone nation in hopes of getting horses and aid in crossing the mountains and the Columbia River. Sacagawea had been raised as a Shoshone, and her brother Cameahwait was now a Shoshone chief. He and Sacagawea were shocked and excited to see each other again, and Lewis was moved by their reunion. But he was more interested in the relations between the Shoshone and tribes to the east as well as Spanish traders to the south.

can discover that these people are by no means friendly to the Spaniards. Their complaint is, that the Spaniards will not let them have fire arms and amunition, that they put them off by telling them that if they suffer them to have guns they will kill each other, thus leaving them defenceless and an easy prey to their bloodthirsty neighbours to the East of them, who being in possession of fire arms hunt them up and murder them without rispect to sex or age and plunder them of their horses on all occasions. They told me that to avoid their enemies who were eternally harrassing them that they were obliged to remain in the interior of these mountains at least two thirds of the year where the[y] suffered as we then saw great heardships for the want of food sometimes living for weeks without meat and only a little fish roots and berries. But this added Câmeahwait, with his ferce eyes and lank jaws grown meager for the want of food, would not be the case if we had guns, we could then live in the country of buffaloe and eat as our enimies do and not be compelled to hide ourselves in these mountains and live on roots and berries as the bear do. We do not fear our enimies when placed on an equal footing with them. I told them that the Minnetares Mandans & Recares of the Missouri had promised us to desist from making war on them & that we would indevour to find the means of making the Minnetares . . . or as they call them Pahkees desist from waging war against them also. That after our finally returning to our homes towards the rising sun whitemen would come to them with an abundance of guns and every other article necessary to their defence and comfort, and that they would be enabled to supply themselves with these articles on reasonable terms in exchange for the skins of the beaver Otter and Ermin so abundant in their country. They expressed great pleasure at this information and said they had been long anxious to see the whitemen that traded guns; and that we might rest assured of their friendship and that they would do whatever we wished them.

Source: Reuben Gold Thwaites, ed., *Original Journals of the Lewis and Clark Expedition, 1804–1808* (New York: Dodd, Mead, 1904), 383–84.

## Interpret the Evidence

1. How do European traders and American explorers view the connection between trade with and peaceful relations among Indian nations (Documents 8.5 and 8.6)?

2. After only a month living near the Mandan, how does William Clark describe relations among Indian nations in the region (Document 8.7)?

3. What are the effects of Lewis and Clark's willingness to trade war hatchets for food, and how does this fit with their desire for peace among the Mandan, Arikara, and other Indian nations (Documents 8.8 and 8.9)?

4. What does Lewis's willingness to promise guns to the Shoshone suggest about the Corps' purpose as it encounters Indian nations living in the Spanish commercial sphere (Document 8.9)?

5. Although these sources were written by white men, what can they tell us about Indian attitudes toward European traders and American explorers and their relations with other Indian nations (Documents 8.5 to 8.9)?

## Put It in Context

What were the most significant problems faced by Indians as more European and American explorers and traders entered the region explored by the Corps of Discovery?

How did the Corps of Discovery influence relations among Indian nations in the West and with the United States?

# Depression, Dissent, and the New Deal

## 1929–1940

### A Sharecropper's Family in Washington County, Arkansas, 1935

Photographers captured ordinary Americans as they tried to survive the hardships of the Great Depression. Through stark black-and-white photos they gave representation to those "forgotten Americans" who were, as Franklin Roosevelt put it, "ill-housed, ill-clad, ill-nourished." ▸ To discover more about what this primary source can show us, see Document 22.7 on page 750.

Franklin D. Roosevelt Library

After reading this chapter you should be able to:

- Describe the Hoover administration's response to the Great Depression and its impact on the rural poor, working people, and minorities.

- Identify the major New Deal programs and assess their positive and negative effects on the groups they were designed to help.

- Explain how the New Deal expanded its scope after 1935 and why it came to an end in 1938.

## AMERICAN HISTORIES

In 1901, at the age of fifteen, Anna Eleanor Roosevelt saw her uncle Theodore succeed William McKinley as president. Like other girls of her generation, Eleanor was expected to marry and become a "charming wife." Eleanor appeared well on her way toward doing so when she married her distant cousin Franklin Delano Roosevelt in 1905. Over a ten-year period, Eleanor gave birth to six children, further reinforcing her status as a traditional woman of her class.

Two events, however, altered the expected course of her life. First, thirteen years into her marriage Eleanor discovered that her husband was having an affair with her social secretary, Lucy Mercer. She did not divorce him but made it clear that she would stay with him primarily as a mother to their children and a political partner. Second, in 1921 Franklin contracted polio. Although he recovered, he would never walk again or stand without the aid of braces. This physical hardship allowed Eleanor to gain increased political influence with Franklin. After her husband won the presidency in 1932, Eleanor did not function as a typical First Lady. She played a very public role promoting her husband's agenda, and she also took advantage of her own extensive contacts in labor unions, civil rights organizations, and women's groups to advance a variety of causes. In many ways more liberal than her husband, Eleanor was a fierce advocate for the rights of women, minorities, workers, and the poor. Behind the scenes, she pushed her husband to move further to the political left.

Eleanor Roosevelt's proximity to power provided her with a unique position from which to confront the problems of her day. In contrast, Luisa Moreno provides a striking example of an activist whose American story bears little resemblance to that of Roosevelt. A native of Guatemala, Moreno moved to Mexico and then New York City. In the midst of the Great Depression, she worked as a seamstress in a sweatshop to support her young child and unemployed husband. Like tens of thousands of people disillusioned with capitalism, in 1930 she joined the Communist Party but quit several years later.

In 1935 Moreno went to Florida to organize cigar workers for the American Federation of Labor (AFL). Despite numerous successes, she grew tired of the AFL's refusal to recruit unskilled workers and jumped to the United Cannery, Agricultural, Packing, and Allied Workers of America (UCAPAWA), an affiliate of the Congress of Industrial Organizations (CIO).

Moreno also promoted the advancement of Latinos throughout the United States. In 1939 she helped create El Congreso de Pueblos de Habla Española (The Congress of Spanish-Speaking People). Besides championing equal access to jobs, education, housing, and health care, the organization pressed to end the segregation of Latinos in schools and public accommodations. Moreno was not nearly as well known as Eleanor Roosevelt, but she worked just as hard to fight poverty, exploitation, and racial bigotry on behalf of people whom President Franklin Roosevelt called "the forgotten Americans." ■

(*left*) **Eleanor Roosevelt**. Library of Congress, 3c08091

(*right*) **Luisa Moreno**. Courtesy of Vicki L. Ruiz

The American histories of Eleanor Roosevelt and Luisa Moreno are very different; both of their lives were shaped in fundamental ways by the same global catastrophe, the Great Depression. Even before the Great Depression, most Americans lived at or near the poverty level, surviving month to month. By 1933, millions of Americans had lost even this tenuous hold on economic security, as unemployment reached a record 25 percent. The Republican administration of President Herbert Hoover depended on private charity and voluntary efforts to meet the needs of downtrodden Americans afflicted by the Depression, but these efforts fell short of the vast need that grew during the Depression and left many frustrated. Proclaiming the establishment of a New Deal for America, Franklin Roosevelt expanded the power of the federal government by initiating relief, recovery, and reform measures, all the while drawing critics on the political left and right. In seeking to break from the past, Roosevelt occasionally overextended his reach, as he did in challenging the Supreme Court. Despite its successes, the New Deal did not end the depression and left minorities and the rural and urban poor still suffering.

# The **Great Depression**

Herbert Hoover had the unenviable task of assuming the presidency in 1929 as the economy crumbled. Given his long history of public service, he seemed the right man for the job. Hoover, however, was unwilling to make a fundamental break with conventional economic approaches and proved unable to effectively communicate his genuine concern for the plight of the poor. Despite his sincere efforts, the depression deepened. As this happened, many Americans, made desperate by their economic plight and angered by the inadequate response of their government, took to the streets in protest.

**Hoover Faces the Depression.** National prosperity was at its peak when the Republican Hoover entered the White House in March 1929. Hoover brought to the presidency a blend of traditional and progressive ideas. He believed that government and business should form voluntary partnerships to work toward common goals. Rejecting the principle of absolute laissez-faire, he nonetheless argued that the government should extend its influence lightly over the economy—to encourage and persuade sensible behavior, but not to impose itself on the private sector.

The Great Depression sorely tested Hoover's beliefs. Having placed his faith in cooperation rather than coercion, the president relied on voluntarism to get the nation through hard economic times. Hoover hoped that management and labor, through gentle persuasion, would hold steady on prices and wages. In the meantime, for those in dire need, the president turned to local communities and private charities. Hoover expected municipal and state governments to shoulder the burden of providing relief to the needy, just as they had during previous economic downturns.

Hoover's remedies failed to rally the country back to good economic health. Initially, businesspeople responded positively to the president's request to maintain the status quo, but when the economy did not bounce back, they lost confidence and defected. Nor did local governments and private agencies have the funds to provide relief to all those who needed it. With tax revenues in decline, some 1,300 municipalities across the country had gone bankrupt by 1933. Benevolent societies and religious groups could handle short-term

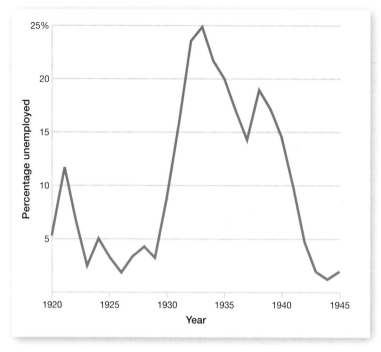

**FIGURE 22.1    Unemployment, 1920–1945**

Business prosperity and immigration restriction ensured low unemployment during most of the 1920s. When unemployment rose dramatically in the late 1920s, President Hoover failed to handle the crisis. During the 1930s, President Roosevelt's New Deal initiatives did lower unemployment to some extent. Still, only mobilizing the nation for war in 1941 created a significant increase in jobs.

misfortunes, but they could not cope with the ongoing disaster of mass unemployment (Figure 22.1).

As confidence in recovery fell and the economy sank deeper into depression, President Hoover shifted direction. He persuaded Congress to lower income tax rates and to allocate an unprecedented $423 million for federal public works projects. In 1929 the president signed into law the Agricultural Marketing Act, a measure aimed at raising prices for long-suffering farmers.

Hoover's recovery efforts fell short, however. He retreated from initiating greater spending because he feared government deficits more than unemployment. With federal accounting sheets showing a rising deficit, Hoover reversed course in 1932 and joined with Congress in sharply raising income, estate, and corporate taxes on the wealthy. This effectively slowed down investment and new production, throwing millions more American workers out of jobs. The Hawley-Smoot Act passed by Congress in 1930 made matters worse. In an effort to replenish revenues and protect American farmers and companies from foreign competition, the act increased tariffs on agricultural and industrial imports. However, other countries retaliated by lifting their import duties, which hurt American companies because it diminished demand for American exports.

In an exception to his aversion to spending, Hoover lobbied Congress to create the Reconstruction Finance Corporation (RFC) to supply loans to troubled banks, railroads, and insurance companies. By injecting federal dollars into these critical enterprises, the president and lawmakers expected to produce dividends that would trickle down from the top of the economic structure to the bottom. In 1932 Congress gave the RFC a budget of

$1.5 billion to employ people in public works projects, a significant allocation for those individuals hardest hit by the depression.

This notable departure from Republican economic philosophy failed to reach its goal. The RFC spent its budget too cautiously, and its funds reached primarily those institutions that could best afford to repay the loans, ignoring the companies in the greatest difficulty. Wealth never trickled down. Although Hoover was not indifferent to the plight of others, he was incapable of breaking away from his ideological preconceptions. He refused to support expenditures for direct relief (what today we call welfare) and hesitated to extend assistance for work relief because he believed that it would ruin individual initiative and character.

Hoover and the United States did not face the Great Depression alone; it was a worldwide calamity. By 1933 Germany, France, and Great Britain were all facing mass unemployment. In this climate of extreme social and economic unrest, authoritarian dictators came to power in a number of European countries, including Germany, Italy, Spain, and Portugal. Each claimed that his country's social and economic problems could be solved only by placing power in the hands of a single, all-powerful leader.

**Hoovervilles and Dust Storms.** The depression hit all areas of the United States hard. In large cities, families crowded into apartments with no gas or electricity and little food to put on the table. In Los Angeles, people cooked their meals over wood fires in backyards. In many cities, the homeless constructed makeshift housing consisting of cartons, old newspapers, and cloth—what journalists derisively dubbed Hoovervilles. Thousands of hungry citizens wound up living under bridges in Portland, Oregon; in wrecked autos in city dumps in Brooklyn, New York, and Stockton, California; and in abandoned coal furnaces in Pittsburgh.

**Soup Kitchen, 1931**  At the height of the Great Depression, these unemployed men stand in a long line outside a Chicago soup kitchen waiting for a meal. Without major government relief efforts for the unemployed during the Hoover administration, such men depended mainly on the efforts of charity. In this instance, the notorious gangster Al Capone set up this establishment before going to federal prison for tax evasion in 1932. National Archives photo no. 306-NT-165319c

Rural workers fared no better. Landlords in West Virginia and Kentucky evicted coal miners and their families from their homes in the dead of winter, forcing them to live in tents. Farmers in the Great Plains, who were already experiencing foreclosures, were little prepared for the even greater natural disaster that laid waste to their farms. In the early 1930s, dust storms swept through western Kansas, eastern Colorado, western Oklahoma, the Texas Panhandle, and eastern New Mexico, in an area that came to be known as the Dust Bowl, destroying crops and plant and animal life. The storms resulted from both climatological and human causes. A series of droughts had destroyed crops and turned the earth into sand, which gusts of wind deposited on everything that lay in their path. Though they did not realize it at the time, plains farmers, by focusing on growing wheat for income, had neglected planting trees and grasses that would have kept the earth from eroding and turning into dust. **See Document Project 22: The Depression in Rural America, page 748.**

As the storms continued through the 1930s, most residents—approximately 75 percent—remained on the plains. Millions, however, headed for California looking for relief from the plague of swirling dirt and hoping to find jobs in the state's fruit and vegetable fields. Although they came from several states besides Oklahoma, these migrants came to be known as "Okies," a derogatory term used by those who resented and looked down on the poverty-stricken newcomers to their communities. John Steinbeck's novel *The Grapes of Wrath* (1939) portrayed the plight of the fictional Joad family as storms and a bank foreclosure destroyed their Oklahoma farm and sent them on the road to California.

### Challenges for Minorities.
Given the demographics of the workforce, the overwhelming majority of Americans who lost their jobs were white men; yet racial and ethnic minorities, including African Americans, Latinos, and Asian Americans, suffered disproportionate hardship. Racial discrimination had kept these groups from achieving economic and political equality, and the Great Depression added to their woes.

Traditionally the last hired and the first fired, blacks occupied the lowest rungs on the industrial and agricultural ladders. "The depression brought everybody down a peg or two," the African American poet Langston Hughes wryly commented. "And the Negroes had but few pegs to fall." Despite the great migration to the North during and after World War I, three-quarters of the black population still lived in the South. Mainly sharecroppers and tenant farmers, black southerners were mired in debt that they could not repay as crop prices plunged to record lows during the 1920s. As white landowners struggled to save their farms by introducing machinery to cut labor costs, they forced black sharecroppers off the land and into even greater poverty. Nor was the situation better for black workers employed at the lowest-paying jobs as janitors, menial laborers, maids, and laundresses. On average, African Americans earned $200 a year, less than one-quarter of the average wage of white factory workers.

The economic misfortune that African Americans experienced was compounded by the fact that they lived in a society rigidly constructed to preserve white supremacy. The 25 percent of blacks living in the North faced racial discrimination in employment, housing, and the criminal justice system, but at least they could express their opinions and desires by voting. By contrast, black southerners remained segregated and disfranchised by law. The depression also exacerbated racial tensions, as whites and blacks competed for the shrinking number of jobs. Lynching, which had declined during the 1920s, surged upward—in 1933 twenty-four blacks lost their lives to this form of terrorism.

**Scottsboro Nine, 1933**   Two years after their original conviction, the Scottsboro defendants discuss their new trial with their attorney Samuel Leibowitz in 1933 while still in prison. Flanked by two guards, they are from the left, Olen Montgomery, Clarence Norris, Willie Roberson, Andrew Wright, Ozie Powell, Eugene Williams, Charlie Weems, and Roy Wright. Haywood Patterson is seated next to Leibowitz. Known as the "Scottsboro Boys," at the time of their arrest, they ranged in age from twelve to nineteen. NYC

Events in Scottsboro, Alabama, reflected the special misery African Americans faced during the Great Depression. Trouble erupted in 1931 when two young, unemployed white women, Ruby Bates and Victoria Price, snuck onto a freight train heading to Huntsville, Alabama. Before the train reached the Scottsboro depot, a fight broke out between black and white men on top of the freight car occupied by the two women. After the train pulled in to Scottsboro, the local sheriff arrested nine black youths between the ages of twelve and nineteen. Charges of assault quickly escalated into rape, when the women told authorities that the black men in custody had molested them on board the train.

The defendants' court-appointed attorney was less than competent and had little time to prepare his clients' cases. It probably made no difference, as the all-white male jury swiftly convicted the accused and awarded the harshest of sentences; only the youngest defendant was not given the death penalty. The Supreme Court spared the lives of the **Scottsboro Nine** by overturning their guilty verdicts in 1932 on the grounds that the defendants did not have adequate legal representation and again in 1935 because blacks had been systematically excluded from the jury pool. Although Ruby Bates had recanted her testimony and there was no physical evidence of rape, retrials in 1936 and 1937 produced the same guilty verdicts, but this time the defendants did not receive the death penalty—a minor victory considering the charges. State prosecutors dismissed charges against four of the accused, all of whom had already spent six years in jail. Despite international protests against this racist injustice, the last of the remaining five did not leave jail until 1950.

**Explore ▶**

See Document 22.1 for a letter from the Scottsboro prisoners.

## GUIDED ANALYSIS

## Plea from the Scottsboro Prisoners, 1932

In 1931, nine black youths were arrested in Scottsboro, Alabama, and charged with raping two white women. They were quickly convicted, and eight were sentenced to death. (One of the nine, Roy Wright, was twelve years old, and the prosecution did not seek the death penalty.) In this letter to the editor of the *Negro Worker*, a Communist magazine, the Scottsboro Nine plead their innocence and ask for help. A year had passed since their arrest and trial, which would account for their ages in the following statement recorded as between thirteen to twenty. Only those sentenced to death signed the letter.

**Document 22.1**

Why do you think they mention their ages?

What tactics did Alabama officials use on the prisoners? What was their purpose?

Why do the Scottsboro prisoners repeatedly emphasize that they were workers?

We have been sentenced to die for something we ain't never done. Us poor boys have been sentenced to burn up on the electric chair for the reason that we is workers—and the color of our skin is black. We like any one of you workers is none of us older than 20. Two of us is 14 and one is 13 years old.

What we guilty of? Nothing but being out of a job. Nothing but looking for work. Our kinfolk was starving for food. We wanted to help them out. So we hopped a freight—just like any one of you workers might a done—to go down to Mobile to hunt work. We was taken off the train by a mob and framed up on rape charges.

At the trial they gave us in Scottsboro we could hear the crowd yelling, "Lynch the Niggers." We could see them toting those big shotguns. Call 'at a fair trial? And while we lay here in jail, the boss-man make us watch 'em burning up other Negroes on the electric chair. "This is what you'll get," they say to us.

Working class boys, we asks you to save us from being burnt on the electric chair. We's only poor working class boys whose skin is black. . . . Help us boys. We ain't done nothing wrong.

[Signed] Andy Wright, Olen Montgomery, Ozie Powell, Charlie Weems, Clarence Norris, Haywood Patterson, Eugene Williams, Willie Robertson

Source: "Scottsboro Boys Appeal from Death Cells to the 'Toilers of the World,'" *The Negro Worker* 2, no. 5 (May 1932): 8–9.

**Put It in Context**

Why was it unlikely that black men in Alabama could receive a fair trial on the charge of raping a white woman?

Racism also worsened the impact of the Great Depression on Spanish-speaking Americans. Mexicans and Mexican Americans made up the largest segment of the Latino population living in the United States. Concentrated in the Southwest and California, they worked in a variety of low-wage factory jobs and as migrant laborers in fruit and vegetable fields. The depression reduced the Mexican-born population living in the United States in two ways. The federal government, in cooperation with state and local governments and private businesses, deported around one million Mexicans, a majority of whom were American citizens. Los Angeles officials organized more than a dozen deportation trains transporting thousands of Mexicans to the border. Many others returned to Mexico voluntarily when demand for labor in the United States dried up. By 1933 the number of repatriations had begun to decline. Fewer migrants came over the border after the depression began in 1929, thereby posing less of an economic threat. In addition the Roosevelt administration adopted more humane policies, attempting not to break up families.

Those who remained endured growing hardships. Relief agencies refused to provide them with the same benefits as whites. Like African Americans, they encountered discrimination in public schools, in public accommodations, and at the ballot box. Conditions remained harshest for migrant workers toiling long hours for little pay and living in overcrowded and poorly constructed housing. In both fields and factories employers had little incentive to improve the situation because there were plenty of white migrant workers to fill their positions.

The transient nature of agricultural work and the vulnerability of Mexican laborers made it difficult for workers to organize, but Mexican American laborers engaged in dozens of strikes in California and Texas in the early 1930s. Most ended in defeat, but a few, such as a strike of pecan shellers in San Antonio, Texas, led by Luisa Moreno, won better working conditions and higher wages. Despite these hard-fought victories, the condition of Latinos remained precarious.

On the West Coast, Asian Americans also remained economically and politically marginalized. Japanese immigrants eked out livings as small farmers, grocers, and gardeners, despite California laws preventing them from owning land. Many of their college-educated U.S.-born children found few professional opportunities available to them, and they often returned to work in family businesses. The depression magnified the problem.

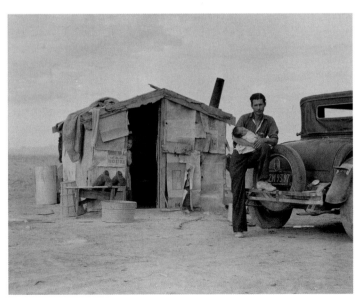

**Mexican Migrant Worker, 1937**
This photograph by Dorothea Lange shows a Mexican field worker on the edge of a frozen pea field in the Imperial Valley, California. Leaning on an automobile, he is holding a baby alongside of a dilapidated shack. Demand for Mexican labor declined during the Great Depression as displaced farmers from the Dust Bowl moved west to take jobs formerly held by Mexicans. Government deportations further decreased the number of undocumented Mexican laborers in the United States. Library of Congress, 8b38632

Like other racial and ethnic minorities, the Japanese found it harder to find even the lowest-wage jobs now that unemployed whites were willing to take them. As a result, about one-fifth of Japanese immigrants returned to Japan during the 1930s.

The Chinese suffered a similar fate. Although some 45 percent of Chinese Americans had been born in the United States and were citizens, people of Chinese ancestry remained isolated in ethnic communities along the West Coast. Discriminated against in schools and most occupations, many operated restaurants and laundries. During the depression, those Chinese who did not obtain assistance through governmental relief turned instead to their own community organizations and to extended families to help them through the hard times.

Filipino immigrants had arrived on the West Coast after the Philippines became a territory of the United States in 1901. Working as low-wage agricultural laborers, they were subject to the same kind of racial animosity as other dark-skinned minorities. Filipino farmworkers organized agricultural labor unions and conducted numerous strikes in California, but like their Mexican counterparts they were brutally repressed. In 1934 anti-Filipino hostility reached its height when Congress passed the Tydings-McDuffie Act. The measure accomplished two aims at once: The act granted independence to the Philippines, and it restricted Filipino immigration into the United States.

### Families under Strain.
With millions of men unemployed, women faced increased family responsibilities. Stay-at-home wives had to care for their children and provide emotional support for out-of-work husbands who had lost their role as the family breadwinner. Despite the loss of income, homemakers continued their daily routines of shopping, cooking, cleaning, and child rearing.

Disproportionate male unemployment led to an increase in the importance of women's income. The depression hit male-dominated industries like steel mills and automakers the hardest. As a result, men were more likely to lose their jobs than women. Although more women held on to their jobs, their often meager wages had to go further because many now had to support unemployed fathers and husbands. During the 1930s, federal and local governments sought to increase male employment by passing laws to keep married women from holding civil service and teaching positions. Nonetheless, more and more married women entered the workplace, and by 1940 the proportion of women in the job force had grown by about 25 percent.

As had been the case in previous decades, a higher proportion of African American women than white women worked outside the home in the 1930s. By 1940 about 40 percent of African American women held jobs, compared to about 25 percent of white women. Racial discrimination played a key role in establishing this pattern. Black men faced higher unemployment rates than did their white counterparts, and what work was available was often limited to the lowest-paying jobs. As a result, black women faced greater pressure to supplement family incomes. Still, unemployment rates for black women reached as high as 50 percent during the 1930s.

Despite increased burdens, most American families remained intact and discovered ways to survive the economic crisis. They pared down household budgets, made do without telephones and new clothes, and held on to their automobiles for longer periods of time. What money they managed to save they often spent on movies. Comedies, gangster movies, fantasy tales, and uplifting films helped viewers forget their troubles, if only for a few hours. Radio remained the chief source of entertainment, and radio sales doubled in the 1930s as listeners tuned in to soap operas, comedy and adventure shows, news reports, and musical programs.

**Organized Protest.** As the depression deepened, angry citizens found ways to express their discontent. Farmers had suffered economic hardship longer than any other group. Even before 1929, they had seen prices spiral downward, but in the early 1930s agricultural income plummeted 60 percent, and one-third of farmers lost their land (Figure 22.2). Some farmers decided that the time had come for drastic action. In the summer of 1932, Milo Reno, an Iowa farmer, created the Farm Holiday Association to organize farmers to keep their produce from going to market and thereby raise prices. Strikers from the association blocked roads and kept reluctant farmers in line by smashing their truck windshields and headlights and slashing their tires. When law enforcement officials arrested fifty-five demonstrators in Council Bluffs, thousands of farmers marched on the jail and forced their release. Despite armed attempts to prevent foreclosures and the intentional destruction of vast quantities of farm produce, the Farm Holiday Association failed to achieve its goal of raising prices.

Disgruntled urban residents also resorted to protest. Although the Communist Party remained a tiny group of just over 10,000 members in 1932, it played a large role in organizing the dispossessed. In major cities such as New York, Communists set up

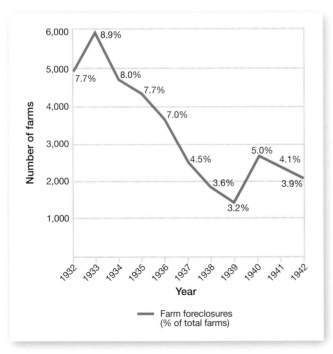

**FIGURE 22.2  Farm Foreclosures, 1932–1942**

A drop of 60 percent in prices led to a wave of farm foreclosures and rural protests in the early 1930s. From 1934 on, federal programs that promoted rural electrification, crop allotments, commodity loans, and mortgage credits allowed many farmers to retain their land. But tenant farmers and sharecroppers, particularly in the South, rarely benefited from these programs.

unemployment councils and led marches and rallies demanding jobs and food. In Harlem, the party endorsed rent strikes by African American apartment residents against their landlords. Party members did not confine their activities to the urban Northeast. They also went south to defend the Scottsboro Nine and to organize industrial workers in the steel mills of Birmingham and sharecroppers in the surrounding rural areas of Alabama. On the West Coast, Communists unionized seamen and waterfront workers and led strikes. They also recruited writers, directors, and actors in Hollywood.

One of the most visible protests of the early 1930s centered on the Ford factory in Dearborn, Michigan. As the depression worsened after 1930, Henry Ford, who had initially pledged to keep employee wages steady, changed his mind and reduced wages. On March 7, 1932, spearheaded by Communists, three thousand autoworkers marched from Detroit to Ford's River Rouge plant in nearby Dearborn. When they reached the factory town, they faced policemen indiscriminately firing bullets and tear gas, which killed four demonstrators. The attack provoked great outrage. Around forty thousand mourners attended the funeral of the four protesters; sang the Communist anthem, the "Internationale"; and surrounded the caskets, which were draped in a red banner emblazoned with a picture of Bolshevik hero Vladimir Lenin.

Protests spread beyond Communist agitators. The federal government faced an uprising by some of the nation's most patriotic and loyal citizens—World War I veterans. Scheduled to receive a $1,000 bonus for their service, unemployed veterans could not wait until the payment date arrived in 1945. Instead, in the spring of 1932 a group of ex-soldiers from Portland, Oregon, set off on a march on Washington, D.C., to demand immediate payment of the bonus by the federal government. By the time they reached the nation's capital, the ranks of this **Bonus Army** had swelled to around twenty thousand veterans. They camped in the Anacostia Flats section of the city, constructed ramshackle shelters, and in many cases moved their families in with them.

Although many veterans returned home, the rest of the Bonus Army remained in place until late July. When President Hoover decided to clear the capital of the protesters, violence ensued. Rather than engaging in a measured and orderly removal, General Douglas MacArthur overstepped presidential orders and used excessive force to disperse the veterans and their families. The Third Cavalry, commanded by George S. Patton, torched tents and sent their residents fleeing from the city.

In this one-sided battle, the biggest loser was President Hoover. Through four years of the country's worst depression, Hoover had lost touch with the American people. His cheerful words of encouragement fell increasingly on deaf ears. As workers, farmers, and veterans stirred in protest, Hoover appeared aloof, standoffish, and insensitive.

## REVIEW & RELATE

- How did President Hoover respond to the problems and challenges created by the Great Depression?

- How did different segments of the American population experience the depression?

# The **New Deal**

The nation was ready for a change, and on election day 1932, with hard times showing no sign of abating, Democratic presidential candidate Franklin Delano Roosevelt defeated Hoover easily. Roosevelt's sizable victory provided him with a mandate to take the country in a bold new direction. However, few Americans, including Roosevelt himself, knew exactly what the new president meant to do or what his pledge of a New Deal would mean for the country.

**Roosevelt Restores Confidence.** As a presidential candidate, Roosevelt presented no clear, coherent policy. He did not spell out how his plans for the country would differ from Hoover's, but he did refer broadly to providing a "new deal" and bringing to the White House "persistent experimentation." Roosevelt's appeal derived more from the genuine compassion he was able to convey than from the specificity of his promises. In this context, Eleanor Roosevelt's evident concern for people's suffering and her history of activism made Franklin Roosevelt even more attractive.

Instead of any fixed ideology, Roosevelt followed what one historian has called "pragmatic humanism." A seasoned politician who understood the need for flexibility, Roosevelt blended principle and practicality. "It is common sense," Roosevelt explained, "to take a method and try it. If it fails, admit it frankly and try another. But above all, try something." More than any president before him, FDR, as he became known, created an expectation among Americans that the federal government would take concrete action to improve their

**Franklin Delano Roosevelt Campaigning in Georgia**   New York governor Franklin Roosevelt greets farmers in Georgia as he campaigns for president in 1932 as the Democratic candidate. Photographers were careful not to show that Roosevelt was unable to use his legs, which were paralyzed after he contracted polio in 1921. Roosevelt forged a coalition of farmers and urban workers and easily defeated the incumbent Hoover. AP Photo lives. A Colorado woman expressed her appreciation to Eleanor Roosevelt: "Your husband is great. He seems lovable even tho' he is a 'politician.'" The New Deal would take its twists and turns, but Roosevelt never lost the support of the majority of Americans.

Starting with his inaugural address, in which he declared that "the only thing we have to fear is fear itself," Roosevelt took on the task of rallying the American people and restoring their confidence in the future. Using the power of radio to communicate directly, Roosevelt delivered regular fireside chats in which he boosted morale and informed his audience of the steps the government was taking to help solve their problems. Not limited to rhetoric, Roosevelt's **New Deal** would provide relief, put millions of people to work, raise prices for farmers, extend conservation projects, revitalize America's financial system, and rescue capitalism.

### Steps toward Recovery.

President Roosevelt took swift action on entering office. In March 1933 he issued an executive order shutting down banks for several days to calm the panic that gripped many Americans in the wake of bank failures and the loss of their life's savings. Shortly after, Congress passed the administration's Emergency Banking Act, which subjected banks to Treasury Department inspection before they reopened, reorganized the banking system, and provided federal funds to bail out banks on the brink of closing. This assertion of federal power allowed solvent banks to reopen. Boosting confidence further, Congress passed the Glass-Steagall Act in June 1933. The measure created the **Federal Deposit Insurance Corporation (FDIC)**, insuring personal savings accounts up to $5,000, and detached commercial banks from investment banks to avoid risky speculation. The president also sought tighter supervision of the stock market. By June 1934 Roosevelt had signed into law measures setting up the Securities and Exchange Commission (SEC) to regulate the stock market and ensure that corporations gave investors accurate information about their portfolios.

The regulation of banks and the stock exchange did not mean that Roosevelt was anti-business. He affirmed his belief in a balanced budget and sought to avoid a $1 billion deficit by cutting government workers' salaries and lowering veterans' pensions. Roosevelt also tried to keep the budget under control by ending prohibition, which would allow the government to tax alcohol sales and eliminate the cost of enforcement. The Twenty-first Amendment, ratified in 1933, ended the more than decade-long experiment with temperance.

As important as these measures were, the Roosevelt administration had much more to accomplish before those hardest hit by the depression felt some relief. Roosevelt viewed the Great Depression as a crisis analogous to war and adapted many of the bureaus and commissions used during World War I to ensure productivity and mobilize popular support to fit the current economic emergency. Many former progressives lined up behind Roosevelt, including women reformers and social workers who had worked in government and private agencies during the 1920s. At his wife Eleanor's urging, Roosevelt appointed one of them, Frances Perkins, as the first woman to head a cabinet agency—the Department of Labor.

Rehabilitating agriculture and industry stood at the top of the New Deal's priority list. Farmers came first. In May 1933 Congress passed the **Agricultural Adjustment Act**, aimed at raising prices by reducing production. The Agricultural Adjustment Administration

(AAA) paid farmers subsidies to produce less in the future, and for farmers who had already planted their crops and raised livestock, the agency paid them to plow under a portion of their harvest, slaughter hogs, and destroy dairy products. By 1935 the program succeeded in raising farm income by 50 percent. Large farmers remained the chief beneficiaries of the AAA because they could afford to cut back production. In doing so, especially in the South, they forced off the land sharecroppers who no longer had plots to farm. Even when sharecroppers managed to retain a parcel of their acreage, AAA subsidies went to the landowners, who did not always distribute the designated funds owed to the sharecroppers. Though poor white farmers felt the sting of this injustice, the system of white supremacy existing in the South guaranteed that blacks suffered most.

The Roosevelt administration exhibited its boldest initiative in creating the **Tennessee Valley Authority (TVA)** in 1933 to bring low-cost electric power to rural areas and help redevelop the entire Tennessee River valley region through flood-control projects. In contrast to the AAA and other farm programs in which control stayed in private hands, the TVA owned and supervised the building and operation of public power plants. For farmers outside the Tennessee River valley, the Rural Electrification Administration helped them obtain cheap electric power starting in 1935, and for the first time tens of thousands of farmers experienced the modern conveniences that electricity brought (though most farmers would not get electric power until after World War II).

Roosevelt and Congress also acted to deal with the soil erosion problem behind the dust storms. In 1933 the Department of Interior established a Soil Erosion Service, and two years later Congress created a permanent Soil Conservation Service in the Department of Agriculture. Although these measures would prove beneficial in the long run, they did nothing to prevent even more severe storms from rolling through the Dust Bowl in 1935 and 1936.

At the same time, Roosevelt concentrated on industrial recovery. In 1933 Congress passed the National Industrial Recovery Act, which established the **National Recovery Administration (NRA)**. This agency allowed business, labor, and the public (represented by government officials) to create codes to regulate production, prices, wages, hours, and collective bargaining. Designers of the NRA expected that if wages rose and prices remained stable, consumer purchasing power would climb, demand would grow, and businesses would put people back to work. For this plan to work, businesspeople needed to keep prices steady by absorbing some of the costs of higher wages. Businesses that joined the NRA displayed the symbol of the blue eagle to signal their patriotic participation.

However, the NRA did not function as planned, nor did it bring the desired recovery. Businesses did not exercise the necessary restraint to keep prices steady. Large manufacturers dominated the code-making committees, and because Roosevelt had suspended enforcement of the antitrust law, they could not resist taking collective action to force smaller firms out of business. The NRA legislation guaranteed labor the right to unionize, but the agency did not vigorously enforce collective bargaining. The government failed to intervene to redress the imbalance of power between labor and management because Roosevelt depended primarily on big business to generate economic improvement. Moreover, the NRA had created codes for too many businesses, and government officials could not properly oversee them all. In 1935 the Supreme Court delivered the final blow to the NRA by declaring it an unconstitutional delegation of legislative power to the president.

**National Recovery Administration Eagles**    President Roosevelt initiated the National Recovery Administration in 1933 as the centerpiece of his New Deal to stimulate economic growth. The city of Miami Beach employed these bathing beauties to attract conventioneers and vacationers to its hotels. Under the NRA code, they worked a forty-hour week and showed their satisfaction by sporting the NRA blue eagle insignia on their backs. © Bettmann/CORBIS

**Direct Assistance and Relief.**  Economic recovery programs were important, but they took time to take effect, and many Americans needed immediate help. Thus relief efforts and direct job creation were critical parts of the New Deal. Created in the early months of Roosevelt's term, the Federal Emergency Relief Administration (FERA) provided cash grants to states to revive their bankrupt relief efforts. Roosevelt chose Harry Hopkins, the chief of New York's relief agency, to head the FERA and distribute its initial $500 million appropriation. On the job for two hours, Hopkins had already spent $5 million. He did not calculate whether a particular plan "would work out in the long run," because, as he remarked, "people don't eat in the long run—they eat every day."

Harold Ickes, secretary of the interior and director of the Public Works Administration (PWA), oversaw efforts to rebuild the nation's infrastructure. Funding architects, engineers, and skilled workers, the PWA built the Grand Coulee, Boulder, and Bonneville dams in the West; the Triborough Bridge in New York City; 70 percent of all new schools constructed between 1933 and 1939; and a variety of municipal buildings, sewage plants, port facilities, and hospitals.

Yet neither the FERA nor the PWA provided enough relief to the millions who faced the winter of 1933–1934 without jobs or the money to heat their homes. In response,

**Explore ▶**

See Documents 22.2 and
22.3 for two views of direct
relief.

Hopkins persuaded Roosevelt to launch a temporary program to help needy Americans get through this difficult period. Both men favored "work relief"— giving people jobs rather than direct welfare payments whenever practical. The Civil Works Administration (CWA) lasted four months, but in that brief time it employed more than 4 million people on about 400,000 projects that built 500,000 miles of roads, 40,000 schools, 3,500 playgrounds, and 1,000 airports.

One of Roosevelt's most successful relief programs was the **Civilian Conservation Corps (CCC)**, created shortly after he entered the White House. The CCC recruited unmarried men between the ages of eighteen and twenty-five for a two-year stint, putting them to work planting forests; cleaning up beaches, rivers, and parks; and building bridges and dams. Participants received $1 per day, and the government sent $25 of the $30 in monthly wages directly to their families, helping make this the most popular of all New Deal programs. The CCC employed around 2.5 million men and lasted until 1942.

**New Deal Critics.** Despite the unprecedented efforts of the Roosevelt administration to spark recovery, provide relief, and encourage reform between 1933 and 1935, the country remained in depression, and unemployment still hovered around 20 percent. Roosevelt found himself under attack from both the left and the right. On the right, conservatives questioned New Deal spending and the growth of big government. On the left, the president's critics argued that he had not done enough to topple wealthy corporate leaders from power and relieve the plight of the downtrodden.

In 1934 officials of the Du Pont Corporation and General Motors formed the American Liberty League. From the point of view of the league's founders, the New Deal was little more than a vehicle for the spread of socialism and communism. The organization spent $1 million attacking what it considered to be Roosevelt's "dictatorial" policies and his assaults on free enterprise. The league, however, failed to attract support beyond a small group of northern industrialists, Wall Street bankers, and disaffected Democrats.

Corporate leaders also harnessed Christian ministers to promote their pro-capitalism, anti–New Deal message. The United States Chamber of Commerce and the National Association of Manufacturers allied with clergymen to challenge "creeping socialism." In 1935 the Reverend James W. Fifield founded Spiritual Mobilization and, from the pulpit of his wealthy First Congregational Church in Los Angeles, praised capitalism as a pillar of Christianity and attacked the "pagan statism" of the New Deal.

Roosevelt also faced criticism from the left. Communist Party membership reached its peak of around 75,000 in 1938, and though the party remained relatively small in numbers, it attracted intellectuals and artists whose voices could reach the larger public. Party members led unionizing drives in both the North and the South and displayed great talent and energy in organizing workers where resistance to unions was greatest. In the mid-1930s, the party followed the Soviet Union's antifascist foreign policy and joined with left-leaning, non-Communist groups, such as unions and civil rights organizations, to oppose the growing menace of fascism in Europe, particularly in Germany and Italy. By the end of the decade, however, the party had lost many members after the Soviet Union reversed its anti-Nazi foreign policy.

The greatest challenge to Roosevelt came from a trio of talented men who reflected diverse beliefs. Francis Townsend, a retired California physician, proposed a "Cure for

**COMPARATIVE ANALYSIS**

# Letters to Eleanor Roosevelt

During the 1930s Americans wrote to President Roosevelt and the First Lady in unprecedented numbers, revealing their personal desperation and their belief that the Roosevelts would respond to their individual pleas. Though most requested government assistance, not all letter writers favored the New Deal. In the following letters written to Eleanor Roosevelt, a high school girl from Albertville, Alabama, asks the First Lady for personal help, while Minnie Hardin of Columbus, Indiana, expresses her frustration with direct relief programs.

**Document 22.2**

## Mildred Isbell to Mrs. Roosevelt, January 1, 1936

Dear Mrs. Roosevelt,

My life has been a story to me and most of the time a miserable one. When I was 7 years old my father left for a law school and never returned. This leaving my mother and 4 children. He left us a small farm, but it could not keep us up. For when we went back to mother's people the renters would not give us part, and we were still dependent. I have been shoved to pillar to post that I feel very relieved to get off to my self.

I am now 15 years old and in the 10th grade. I have always been smart but I never had a chance as all of us is so poor. I hope to complete my education, but I will have to quit school I guess if there is no clothes can be bought. (Don't think that we are on the relief.) Mother has been a faithful servent for us to keep us to gather. I don't see how she has made it.

Mrs Roosevelt, don't think I am just begging, but that is all you can call it I guess. There is no harm in asking I guess eather. Do you have any old clothes you have throwed back. You don't realize how honored I would feel to be wearing your clothes. I don't have a coat at all to wear. The clothes may be too large but I can cut them down so I can wear them. Not only clothes but old shoes, hats, hose, and under wear would be appreciated so much. I have three brothers that would appreciate any old clothes of your boys or husband. I wish you could see the part of North Alabama now. The trees, groves, and every thing is covered with ice and snow. It is a very pretty scene. But Oh, how cold it is here. People can hardly stay comfortable.

Sources: Mildred Isbell, letter to Eleanor Roosevelt, January 1, 1936; Minnie Hardin, letter to Eleanor Roosevelt, December 14, 1937, Eleanor Roosevelt Papers, Series 190, Miscellaneous, 1937, Franklin D. Roosevelt Library.

Depressions." In 1934 he formed the Old-Age Revolving Pensions Corporation, whose title summed up the doctor's idea. Townsend would have the government give all Americans over the age of sixty a monthly pension of $200 if they retired and spent the entire stipend each month. Retirements would open up jobs for younger workers, and the income these workers received, along with the pension for the elderly, would pump ample funds into the economy to promote recovery. The government would fund the Townsend plan with a 2 percent "transaction" or sales tax. By 1936 Townsend Clubs had attracted about

## Minnie Hardin to Mrs. Roosevelt, December 14, 1937

Mrs. Roosevelt:

I suppose from your point of view the work relief, old age pensions, slum clearance, and all the rest seems like a perfect remedy for all the ills of this country, but I would like for you to see the results, as the other half see them.

We have always had a shiftless, never-do-well class of people whose one and only aim in life is to live without work. I have been rubbing elbows with this class for nearly sixty years and have tried to help some of the most promising and have seen others try to help them, but it can't be done. We cannot help those who will not try to help themselves and if they do try, a square deal is all they need, and by the way that is all this country needs or ever has needed: a square deal for all and then, let each paddle their own canoe, or sink.

There has never been any necessity for any one who is able to work, being on relief in this locality, but there have been many eating the bread of charity and they have lived better than ever before. I have had taxpayers tell me that their children came from school and asked why they couldn't have nice lunches like the children on relief. The women and children around here have had to work at the fields to help save the crops and several women fainted while at work and at the same time we couldn't go up or down the road without stumbling over some of the reliefers, moping around carrying dirt from one side of the road to the other and back again, or else asleep.

### Interpret the Evidence

1. How does each writer explain the source of poverty and the attitudes of poor people?
2. If Minnie Hardin were answering Mildred Isbell's letter, what would she say to her?

### Put It in Context

How did the New Deal tackle poverty?

3.5 million members throughout the country, and one-fifth of all adults in the United States signed a petition endorsing the Townsend plan.

While Townsend appealed mainly to the elderly, Charles E. Coughlin, a priest from the Detroit area, attracted Catholics and a lower-middle-class following. Father Coughlin used his popular national radio broadcasts to talk about economic and political issues. Originally a Roosevelt supporter, by 1934 Coughlin had begun criticizing the New Deal for catering to greedy bankers. He spoke to millions of radio listeners about the evils of the

**Father Charles E. Coughlin** Father Charles E. Coughlin spoke at Cleveland Stadium in 1936 on behalf of Ohio congressional candidates who had been endorsed by his National Union for Social Justice. Coughlin, a Catholic priest and a stern critic of President Roosevelt, advocated the nationalization of banks and other industries, protection of worker rights, and monetary reform. Despite Coughlin's outspoken opposition, Roosevelt easily won reelection in 1936.
© Bettman/CORBIS

Roosevelt administration, the godless Communists who had allegedly infested it, and international bankers—coded language referring to Jews—who supposedly manipulated it. As the decade wore on, his strident anti-Semitism and his growing fondness for fascist dictatorships abroad overshadowed his economic justice message, and Catholic officials ordered him to stop broadcasting.

Huey Pierce Long of Louisiana posed the greatest political threat to Roosevelt. Unlike Townsend and Coughlin, Long had built and operated a successful political machine, first as governor and then as U.S. senator, taking on the special interests of oil and railroad corporations in his home state. Early on he had backed Roosevelt, but Long found the New Deal wanting. In 1934 Long established the Share Our Wealth society, promising to make "every man a king" by presenting families with a $5,000 homestead and a guaranteed annual income of $2,000. To accomplish this, Long proposed levying heavy income and inheritance taxes on the wealthy. Although the financial calculations behind his bold plan did not add up, Share Our Wealth clubs counted some seven million members. The swaggering senator departed from most of his segregationist southern colleagues by appealing to a coalition of disgruntled farmers, industrial workers, and African Americans. Before Long could help lead a third-party campaign for president, he was shot and killed in 1935.

## REVIEW & RELATE

● What steps did Roosevelt take to stimulate economic recovery and provide relief to impoverished Americans during his first term in office?

● What criticisms did Roosevelt's opponents level against the New Deal?

# The **New Deal** **Moves** to the **Left**

Facing criticism from within his own party about the pace and effectiveness of the New Deal, and with the 1936 election looming, Roosevelt moved to the left. He adopted harsher rhetoric against recalcitrant corporate leaders; beefed up economic and social programs for the unemployed, the elderly, and the infirm; and revived measures to redress the power imbalance between management and labor. In doing so, he fashioned a New Deal political coalition that would deliver a landslide victory in 1936 and allow the Democratic Party to dominate electoral politics for the next three decades.

**Expanding Relief Measures.** Even though the New Deal had helped millions of people, millions of others still felt left out, as the popularity of Townsend, Coughlin, and Long indicated. "We the people voted for you," a Columbus, Ohio, worker wrote the president in disgust, "but it is a different story now. You have faded out on the masses of hungry, idle people. . . . The very rich is the only one who has benefited from your new deal."

In 1935 the president seized the opportunity to win his way back into the hearts of impoverished "forgotten Americans." Although Roosevelt favored a balanced budget, political necessity forced him to embark on deficit spending to expand the New Deal. Federal government expenditures would now exceed tax revenues, but New Dealers argued that these outlays would stimulate job creation and economic growth, which ultimately would replenish government coffers. Based on the highly successful but short-lived Civil Works Administration, the **Works Progress Administration (WPA)** provided jobs for the unemployed with a far larger budget, starting out with $5 billion. To ensure that the money would be spent, Roosevelt appointed Harry Hopkins to head the agency. Although critics condemned the WPA for employing people on unproductive "make-work" jobs—a criticism not entirely unfounded—overall the WPA did a great deal of good. The agency constructed or repaired more than 100,000 public buildings, 600 airports, 500,000 miles of roads, and 100,000 bridges. The WPA employed about 8.5 million workers during its eight years of operation.

The WPA also helped artists, writers, and musicians. Under its auspices, the Federal Writers Project, the Federal Art Project, the Federal Music Project, and the Federal Theater Project encouraged the production of cultural works and helped bring them to communities and audiences throughout the country. Writers Richard Wright, Ralph Ellison, Clifford Odets, Saul Bellow, John Cheever, Margaret Walker, and many others nourished both their works and their stomachs while employed by the WPA. Some painters, such as Jacob Lawrence, worked in the "easel division"; others created elaborate murals on the walls of post offices and other government buildings. Historians and folklorists researched and prepared city and state guides and interviewed black ex-slaves whose narratives of the system of bondage would otherwise have been lost.

In addition to the WPA, the National Youth Administration (NYA) employed millions of young people. Their work ranged from clerical assignments and repairing automobiles to building tuberculosis isolation units and renovating schools. Heading the NYA in Texas, the young Lyndon B. Johnson worked hard to expand educational and construction projects to unemployed whites and blacks. The Division of Negro Affairs, headed by the Florida educator Mary McLeod Bethune and the only minority group subsection in the NYA, ensured that African American youths would benefit from the programs sponsored by the agency.

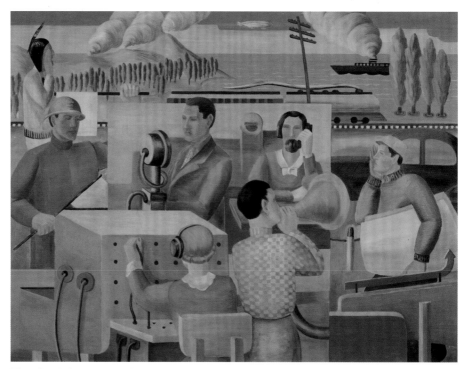

**New Deal Art**   The Works Progress Administration, established by the Roosevelt administration in 1935, put Americans to work amid the ongoing depression. The WPA's Federal Art Project employed artists such as Ingrid E. Edwards of Minnesota, whose painting *Communications* features a newspaper boy, a telephone operator, a radio announcer, and a railroad train. Many of these works adorned public buildings. Collection of Minnesota Historical Society. Lent by Fine Arts Collection, Public Buildings Service, U.S. General Services. Gift of Ah-Gwah Ching Archive

Despite their many successes, these relief programs had a number of flaws. The WPA paid participants relatively low wages. The $660 in annual income earned by the average worker fell short of the $1,200 that a family needed to survive. In addition, the WPA limited participation to one family member. In most cases, this meant the male head of the household. As a result, women made up only about 14 percent of WPA workers, and even in the peak year of 1938, the WPA hired only 60 percent of eligible women. With the exception of the program for artists, most women hired by the WPA worked in lower-paying jobs than men.

**Establishing Social Security.**  The elderly required immediate relief and insurance in a country that lagged behind the rest of the industrialized world in helping its aged workforce. In August 1935, the president rectified this shortcoming and signed into law the **Social Security Act**. The measure provided that at age sixty-five, eligible workers would receive retirement payments funded by payroll taxes on employees and employers. The law also extended beyond the elderly by providing unemployment insurance for those temporarily laid off from work and welfare payments for the disabled who were permanently out of a job as well as for destitute, dependent children of single parents.

**TABLE 22.1   Major New Deal Measures, 1933–1938**

| Year | Legislation | Purpose |
|------|-------------|---------|
| 1933 | National Industrial Recovery Act | Government, business, labor cooperation to set prices, wages, and production codes |
|      | Agricultural Adjustment Act | Paid farmers to reduce production to raise prices |
|      | Civilian Conservation Corps | Jobs for young men in conservation |
|      | Public Works Administration | Construction jobs for the unemployed |
|      | Federal Emergency Relief Act | Relief funds for the poor |
|      | Tennessee Valley Authority | Electric power and flood control to rural areas |
|      | Glass-Steagall Act | Insured bank deposits and separated commercial from investment banking |
| 1934 | Securities and Exchange Commission | Regulated the stock market |
| 1935 | Social Security Act | Provided retirement pensions, unemployment insurance, aid to the disabled, and payments to women with dependent children |
|      | Wagner Act | Guaranteed collective bargaining for unions |
|      | Works Progress Administration | Provided jobs to 8 million unemployed |
| 1938 | Fair Labor Standards Act | Established minimum hourly wage and maximum weekly working hours |

The Social Security program had significant limitations. The act excluded farm, domestic, and laundry workers, who were among the neediest Americans and were disproportionately African American. The reasons for these exclusions were largely political. The president needed southern Democrats to support this measure, and as a Mississippi newspaper observed: "The average Mississippian can't imagine himself chipping in to pay pensions for able bodied Negroes to sit around in idleness." The system of financing pensions also proved unfair. The payroll tax, which imposed the same fixed percentage on all incomes, was a regressive tax, one that fell hardest on those with lower incomes. Nor did Social Security take into account the unpaid labor of women who remained in the home to take care of their children.

Even with its flaws, Social Security revolutionized the expectations of American workers. It created a compact between the federal government and its citizens, and workers insisted that their political leaders fulfill their moral responsibilities to keep the system going. President Roosevelt recognized that the tax formula might not be economically sound, but he had a higher political objective in mind. He believed that payroll taxes would give contributors the right to collect their benefits and that "with those taxes in there, no damn politician can ever scrap my social security program."

**Organized Labor Strikes Back.** In 1935 Congress passed the **National Labor Relations Act**, also known as the Wagner Act for its leading sponsor, Senator Robert F. Wagner Sr. of New York. The law created the National Labor Relations Board (NLRB),

**Women's Emergency Brigade, 1937** After the United Auto Workers initiated a sit-down strike against General Motors in Flint, Michigan, for union recognition, better working conditions, and higher wages, a group of their women relatives, friends, and coworkers formed the Women's Emergency Brigade. In this February 1937 demonstration, they held the clubs that they had used to smash windows at the Chevrolet Plant occupied by the strikers. AP Photo

which protected workers' right to organize labor unions without owner interference. During the 1930s, union membership rolls soared from fewer than 4 million workers to more than 10 million, including more than 800,000 women. At the outset of the depression, barely 6 percent of the labor force belonged to unions, compared with 33 percent in 1940.

Government efforts boosted this growth, but these spectacular gains were due primarily to workers' grassroots efforts set in motion by economic hard times. The number of striking workers during the first year of the Roosevelt administration soared from nearly 325,000 to more than 1.5 million. Organizers such as Luisa Moreno traveled the country to bring as many people as possible into the union movement. The most important development within the labor movement occurred in 1935, with the creation of the CIO. After the AFL, which consisted mainly of craft unions, rejected a proposal by John L. Lewis of the United Mine Workers to incorporate industrial workers under its umbrella, Lewis and representatives of seven other AFL unions defected and formed the CIO. Unlike the AFL, the new union sought to recruit a wide variety of workers without respect to race, gender, or region.

In 1937 the CIO mounted a full-scale organizing campaign. More than 4.5 million workers participated in some 4,700 strikes. Unions found new ways to protest poor working conditions and arbitrary layoffs. Members of the United Auto Workers (UAW), a CIO affiliate, launched a **sit-down strike** against General Motors (GM) in Flint, Michigan, to win union recognition, higher wages, and better working conditions. Strikers refused to work but remained in the plants, shutting them down from the inside. When the company sent in local police forces to evict the strikers on January 11, 1937, the barricaded workers bombarded the police with spare machine parts and anything that was not bolted down. The community rallied around the strikers, and wives and daughters called "union maids" formed the Women's Emergency Brigade, which supplied sit-downers with food and water and kept up their morale. Neither the state nor the federal government interfered with the work stoppage, and after six weeks GM acknowledged defeat and recognized the UAW.

The following year, the New Deal added a final piece of legislation sought by organized labor. The **Fair Labor Standards Act** (1938) established minimum wages at 40 cents an hour and maximum working hours at forty per week. By the end of the decade "big labor," as the AFL and CIO unions were known, had become a significant force in American politics and a leading backer of the New Deal.

**A Half Deal for Minorities.** President Roosevelt made significant gestures on behalf of African Americans. He appointed Mary McLeod Bethune and Robert Weaver to staff New Deal agencies and gathered an informal "Black Cabinet" in the nation's capital to advise him on matters pertaining to race. The Roosevelt administration also established the Civil Liberties Unit (later renamed Civil Rights Section) in the Department of Justice, which investigated racial discrimination. Eleanor Roosevelt acted as a visible symbol of the White House's concern with the plight of blacks. In 1939 Eleanor Roosevelt quit the Daughters of the American Revolution, a women's organization, when it refused to allow black singer Marian Anderson to hold a concert in Constitution Hall in Washington, D.C. Instead, the First Lady brought Anderson to sing on the steps of the Lincoln Memorial.

Perhaps the greatest measure of Franklin Roosevelt's impact on African Americans came when large numbers of black voters switched from the Republican to the Democratic Party in 1936, a pattern that has lasted to the present day. "Go turn Lincoln's picture to the wall," a black observer commented after the election. "That debt has been paid in full."

Yet overall the New Deal did little to break down racial inequality. President Roosevelt believed that the plight of African Americans would improve, along with that of all down-trodden Americans, as New Deal measures restored economic health. Black leaders disagreed. They argued that the NRA's initials stood for "Negroes Ruined Again" because the agency displaced black workers and approved lower wages for blacks than for whites. The AAA dislodged black sharecroppers. New Deal programs such as the CCC and those for building public housing maintained existing patterns of segregation. Both the Social Security Act and the Fair Labor Standards Act omitted from coverage jobs that black Americans were most likely to hold. In fact, the New Deal's big labor/big government alliance left out non-unionized industrial and agricultural workers, many of whom were African American and lacked bargaining power.

This pattern of halfway reform persisted for other minorities. Since the end of the Indian wars in 1890, Native Americans had lived in poverty, forced onto reservations where they were offered few economic opportunities and where whites carried out a relentless assault on their culture. By the early 1930s, American Indians earned an average income of less than $50 a year—compared with $800 for whites—and their unemployment

**The Indian New Deal**    John Collier, commissioner of Indian affairs under President Roosevelt, favored a New Deal for Native Americans. An advocate for Indian culture, Collier implemented reform legislation that replaced the policy of Indian assimilation with that of self-determination. In this 1935 photograph, Collier watches his boss, Secretary of the Interior Harold Ickes, sign the Flathead (Montana) Indian Constitution as tribal leaders look on. © Bettmann/CORBIS

rate was three times higher than that of white Americans. For the most part, they lived on lands that whites had given up on as unsuitable for farming or mining. The policy of assimilation established by the Dawes Act of 1887 had exacerbated the problem by depriving Indians of their cultural identities as well as their economic livelihoods. In 1934 the federal government reversed its course. Spurred on by John Collier, the commissioner of Indian affairs, Congress passed the **Indian Reorganization Act (IRA)**, which terminated the Dawes Act, authorized self-government for those living on reservations, extended tribal landholdings, and pledged to uphold native customs and language.

Although the IRA brought economic and social improvements for Native Americans, many problems remained. Despite his considerable efforts, Collier approached Indian affairs from the top down. One historian remarked that Collier had "the zeal of a crusader who knew better than the Indians what was good for them." The Indian commissioner failed to appreciate the diversity of native tribes and administered laws that contradicted Native American political and economic practices. For example, the IRA required the tribes to operate by majority rule, whereas many of them reached decisions through consensus, which respected the views of the minority. Although 174 tribes accepted the IRA, 78 tribes, including the Seneca, Crow, and Navajo, rejected it.

**Decline of the New Deal.**    Roosevelt's shift to the left paid political dividends, and in 1936 the president won reelection by a landslide. His sweeping victory proved to be one of the rare critical elections that signified a fundamental political realignment. Democrats replaced Republicans as the majority party in the United States, overturning thirty-six years of Republican rule. While Roosevelt had won convincingly in 1932, not until 1936 did the president put together a stable coalition that could sustain Democratic dominance for many years to come.

In 1936 Roosevelt trounced Alfred M. Landon, the Republican governor of Kansas, and Democrats increased their congressional majorities by staggering margins. The vote broke down along class lines. Roosevelt won the votes of 80 percent of union members, 81 percent of unskilled workers, and 84 percent of people on relief, compared with only 42 percent of high-income voters. Millions of new voters came out to the polls, and most of them supported Roosevelt's New Deal coalition of the poor, farmers, urban ethnic minorities, unionists, white southerners, and African Americans.

The euphoria of his triumph, however, proved short-lived. An overconfident Roosevelt soon reached beyond his electoral mandate and within two years found himself unable to extend the New Deal. In 1937 Roosevelt devised a **court-packing plan** to ensure support of New Deal legislation and asked Congress to increase the size of the Supreme Court. He justified this as a matter of reform, claiming that the present nine-member Court could not handle its workload. Roosevelt attributed a good deal of the problem to the advanced age of six of the nine justices, who were over seventy years old. Under his proposal, the president would make one new appointment for each judge over the age of seventy who did not retire so long as the bench did not exceed fifteen members. In reality, Roosevelt schemed to "pack" the Court with supporters to prevent it from declaring New Deal legislation such as Social Security and the Wagner Act unconstitutional.

> **Explore ▶**
>
> See Document 22.4 for a critique of Roosevelt's court-packing plan.

The plan backfired. Conservatives charged Roosevelt with seeking to destroy the separation of powers enshrined in the Constitution among the executive, legislative, and judicial branches. In the end, the president failed to expand the Supreme Court, but he preserved his legislative accomplishments.

In a series of rulings, the chastened Supreme Court approved Social Security, the Wagner Act, and other New Deal legislation. Nevertheless, the political fallout from the court-packing fight damaged the president and his plans for further legislative reform.

Roosevelt's court-packing plan alienated many southern Democratic members of Congress who previously had sided with the president. Traditionally suspicious of the power of the federal government, southern lawmakers worried that Roosevelt was going too far toward centralizing power in Washington at the expense of states' rights. Southern Democrats formed a coalition with conservative northern Republicans who shared their concerns about the expansion of federal power and excessive spending on social welfare programs. Their antipathy toward labor unions further bound them. Although they held a minority of seats in Congress, this **conservative coalition** could block unwanted legislation by using the filibuster in the Senate (unlimited debate that could be shut down only with a two-thirds vote). After 1938 these conservatives made sure that no further New Deal legislation passed.

Roosevelt also lost support for New Deal initiatives because of the recession of 1937, which FDR's policies had triggered. When federal spending soared after passage of the WPA and other relief measures adopted in 1935, the president lost his economic nerve for deficit spending. He called for reduced spending, which increased unemployment and slowed economic recovery. In addition, as the Social Security payroll tax took effect, it reduced the purchasing power of workers, thereby exacerbating the impact of reduced

**SOLO ANALYSIS**

## Retire or Move Over, 1937

In his first term, President Roosevelt secured legislation to implement his New Deal; however, by 1937 the Supreme Court had overturned several key pieces of New Deal legislation, arguing that Congress had exceeded its constitutional authority. As the Social Security Act and the National Labor Relations Act came up for review before the Court, Roosevelt tried to dilute the influence of the Court's conservative majority. Following his landslide reelection in 1936, he asked Congress to enlarge the Court so that he could appoint justices more favorable to his liberal agenda. This cartoon reacts to Roosevelt's court-packing plan.

**Document 22.4**

Granger, NYC

### Interpret the Evidence

1. How does the cartoonist portray Roosevelt? How does it portray the Supreme Court?
2. How does this cartoon appeal to the fears of the American public during the late 1930s?

### Put It in Context

How important was the Supreme Court in shaping the outcome of the New Deal?

government spending. Making the situation worse, pension payments were not scheduled to begin for several years. This "recession within the depression" further eroded congressional support for the New Deal.

The country was still deep in depression in 1939. Unemployment was at 17 percent, with more than 11 million people out of work. Most of those who were poor at the start of the Great Depression remained poor. Recovery came mainly to those who were temporarily impoverished as a result of the economic crisis. The distribution of wealth remained skewed toward the top. In 1933 the richest 5 percent of the population controlled 31 percent of disposable income; in 1939 the latter figure stood at 26 percent.

Against this backdrop of persistent difficult economic times, the president's popularity began to fade. In the midterm elections of 1938, Roosevelt campaigned against Democratic conservatives in an attempt to reinvigorate his New Deal coalition. His efforts failed and upset many ordinary citizens who associated the tactic with that used by European dictators who had recently risen to power. As the decade came to a close, Roosevelt turned his attention away from the New Deal and increasingly toward a new war in Europe that threatened to engulf the entire world.

### REVIEW & RELATE

- Why and how did the New Deal shift to the left in 1934 and 1935?

- Despite the president's landslide victory in 1936, why did the New Deal stall during Roosevelt's second term in office?

# Conclusion: New Deal Liberalism

The Great Depression produced enormous economic hardships that the Hoover administration fell far short of relieving. Although Hoover's successor, Franklin Roosevelt, also failed to end the depression, in contrast he provided unprecedented economic assistance to the poor as well as the rich. The New Deal expanded the size of the federal government from 605,000 employees to more than 1 million during the 1930s. Moreover, the New Deal rescued the capitalist system, doing little to alter the fundamental structure of the American economy. Despite subjecting businesses to greater regulation, it left corporations, the stock market, farms, and banks in the hands of private enterprise. Indeed, by the end of the 1930s large corporations had more power over markets than ever before. Income and wealth remained unequally distributed, nearly to the same extent as they had been before Roosevelt took office in 1933.

Roosevelt forged a middle path between reactionaries and revolutionaries at a time when the fascist tyrants Adolf Hitler and Benito Mussolini gained power in Germany and Italy, respectively, and Joseph Stalin ruthlessly consolidated his rule in the Communist Soviet Union. By contrast, the American president expanded democratic capitalism, bringing a broader cross section of society to the decision-making table. Roosevelt's "broker state" of multiple competing interests provided for greater democracy than a government dominated exclusively by business elites. This system did not benefit those who remained unorganized and wielded little power, but marginalized groups—African Americans, Latinos, and Native Americans—did receive greater recognition and self-determination from the federal government. Indeed, these and other groups helped shape the New Deal. As Eleanor Roosevelt's history shows, women played key roles in campaigning for social welfare legislation. Others, like Luisa Moreno, helped organize workers and promoted ethnic pride among Latinos in the face of deportations. African Americans challenged racism and pressured the federal government to distribute services more equitably. American Indians won important democratic and cultural reforms, and though Asian Americans continued to encounter considerable discrimination on the West Coast, they joined to help each other. President Roosevelt also solidified the institution of the presidency as the focal point for public leadership. His cheerfulness, hopefulness, and pragmatism rallied millions of individuals behind him. Even after Roosevelt died in 1945, the public retained its expectation that leadership would come from the White House.

Through his programs and his force of personality, Franklin Roosevelt convinced Americans that he cared about their welfare and that the federal government would not ignore their suffering. However, he was not universally beloved: Millions of Americans despised him because they thought he was leading the country toward socialism, and he did not solve all the problems the country faced—it would take government spending for World War II to end the depression. Still, together with his wife, Eleanor, Franklin Roosevelt conveyed a sense that the American people belonged to a single community, capable of banding together to solve the country's problems, no matter how serious they were or how intractable they might seem.

## TIMELINE OF EVENTS

| | |
|---|---|
| **1931** | Scottsboro Nine tried for rape |
| **1932–1939** | Dust Bowl storms |
| **1932** | Reconstruction Finance Corporation created |
| | River Rouge autoworkers' strike |
| | Farm Holiday Association formed |
| | Bonus Army marches |
| **1933** | Roosevelt moves to stabilize banking and financial systems |
| | Agricultural Adjustment Act passed |
| | Federal Emergency Relief Administration created |
| | Tennessee Valley Authority created |
| | National Recovery Administration created |
| | Civilian Conservation Corps created |
| **1934** | Indian Reorganization Act passed |
| | Francis Townsend forms Old-Age Revolving Pensions Corporation |
| | Huey Long establishes Share Our Wealth movement |
| | Securities and Exchange Commission created |
| **1935** | Charles E. Coughlin organizes National Union for Social Justice |
| | Works Progress Administration created |
| | Social Security Act passed |
| | National Labor Relations Act passed |
| | Congress of Industrial Organizations founded |
| **1937** | Sit-down strike against General Motors |
| | Roosevelt proposes to increase the size of the Supreme Court |
| **1938** | Fair Labor Standards Act passed |

## KEY TERMS

Scottsboro Nine, *723*

Bonus Army, *728*

New Deal, *730*

Federal Deposit Insurance Corporation (FDIC), *730*

Agricultural Adjustment Act, *730*

Tennessee Valley Authority (TVA), *731*

National Recovery Administration (NRA), *731*

Civilian Conservation Corps (CCC), *733*

Works Progress Administration (WPA), *737*

Social Security Act, *738*

National Labor Relations Act, *739*

sit-down strike, *741*

Fair Labor Standards Act, *741*

Indian Reorganization Act (IRA), *742*

court-packing plan, *743*

conservative coalition, *743*

## REVIEW & RELATE

1. How did President Hoover respond to the problems and challenges created by the Great Depression?
2. How did different segments of the American population experience the depression?
3. What steps did Roosevelt take to stimulate economic recovery and provide relief to impoverished Americans during his first term in office?
4. What criticisms did Roosevelt's opponents level against the New Deal?
5. Why and how did the New Deal shift to the left in 1934 and 1935?
6. Despite the president's landslide victory in 1936, why did the New Deal stall during Roosevelt's second term in office?

# The Depression in Rural America

During the 1930s, rural Americans' lives were devastated by the twin disasters of the Great Depression and, in the Great Plains, the most sustained drought in American history. But both problems only deepened the already difficult problems of many farmers. Agriculture in the South had long been dominated by sharecropping, a system that hampered crop diversification and left many African American tenant farmers vulnerable to exploitation by white landowners. In the Midwest, farmers had spent decades overgrazing pastures and exhausting the soil through overproduction. Prices dropped dramatically throughout the 1920s, and farmers were the only group whose incomes fell during that decade.

When the depression hit, many farmers did not have the resources to stay on their land, and farm foreclosures tripled in the early 1930s. Ferocious dust storms plagued many of the farmers who desperately struggled to hold on to their land (Document 22.5). Sharecroppers, tenant farmers, and former farm owners left their homes to find better opportunities, and a million people left the Great Plains alone (Document 22.7). Many ended up as migrant agricultural laborers in farms and orchards on the West Coast. Feeling overrun by refugees, California passed a law in 1937 making it a misdemeanor to bring into California any indigent person who was not a state resident. This law remained in effect until 1941.

Under the New Deal, the federal government acted in a number of ways to relieve the plight of farmers around the country. The Agricultural Adjustment Act attempted to raise crop prices and stabilize agricultural incomes by encouraging farmers to cut production. In doing so, however, it did little to relieve the plight of African American farmers (Document 22.6). The Farm Credit Act helped some farmers refinance mortgages at a lower rate, the Rural Electrification Administration brought electricity to farm areas previously without it, and the Soil Conservation Service advised farmers on how to properly cultivate their hillsides. The report of the Great Plains Committee (Document 22.9), another Roosevelt creation, detailed additional recommendations for helping the agricultural economy in the Midwest. In contrast, the federal government failed to protect Mexican migrant workers and instead deported a large number of them to Mexico (Document 22.8).

Consider what the following documents reveal about the challenges faced by rural Americans and how different individuals and groups responded to those problems.

## Document 22.5

### Ann Marie Low | Dust Bowl Diary, 1934

When massive dust storms swept through the Midwest beginning in the early 1930s, they blew away the topsoil of a once productive farm region and created hazardous living conditions. Residents needed to clean and wash repetitively to perform even simple daily tasks. Ann Marie Low, a young woman living with her family in southeastern North Dakota, describes the difficulty of life in the Dust Bowl.

*May 21, 1934, Monday . . .*

Saturday Dad, Bud, and I planted an acre of potatoes. There was so much dirt in the air I couldn't see Bud only a few feet in front of me. Even the air in the house was just a haze. In the evening the wind died down, and Cap came to take me to the movie. We

joked about how hard it is to get cleaned up enough
to go anywhere.

The newspapers report that on May 10 there was
such a strong wind the experts in Chicago estimated
12,000,000 tons of Plains soil was dumped on that
city. By the next day the sun was obscured in
Washington, D.C., and ships 300 miles out at sea
reported dust settling on their decks.

Sunday the dust wasn't so bad. Dad and I drove
cattle to the Big Pasture. Then I churned butter and
baked a ham, bread, and cookies for the men, as no
telling when Mama will be back.

*May 30, 1934, Wednesday*

Ethel got along fine, so Mama left her at the hospital
and came to Jamestown by train Friday. Dad took us
both home.

The mess was incredible! Dirt had blown into
the house all week and lay inches deep on
everything. Every towel and curtain was just black.
There wasn't a clean dish or cooking utensil. There
was no food. Oh, there were eggs and milk and one
loaf left of the bread I baked the weekend before. I
looked in the cooler box down the well (our
refrigerator) and found a little ham and butter. It was
late, so Mama and I cooked some ham and eggs for
the men's supper because that was all we could fix in
a hurry. It turned out they had been living on ham
and eggs for two days.

. . . It took until 10 o'clock to wash all the dirty
dishes. That's not wiping them—just washing them.
The cupboards had to be washed out to have a clean
place to put them.

Saturday was a busy day. Before starting
breakfast I had to sweep and wash all the dirt
off the kitchen and dining room floors, wash the
stove, pancake griddle, and dining room table and
chairs. There was cooking, baking, and churning to
be done for those hungry men. Dad is 6 feet 4 inches
tall, with a big frame. Bud is 6 feet 3 inches and
almost as big-boned as Dad. We say feeding them is
like filling a silo.

Mama couldn't make bread until I carried water
to wash the bread mixer. I couldn't churn until the
churn was washed and scalded. We just couldn't
do anything until something was washed first.

Every room had to have dirt almost shoveled out
of it before we could wash floors and furniture.

Source: Ann Marie Low, *Dust Bowl Diary* (Lincoln: University of
Nebraska Press, 1984), 96–97.

Document 22.6

## John P. Davis | A Black Inventory of the New Deal, 1935

African Americans shouldered a double burden
during the Great Depression. Already victims of racial
oppression, they now fell into even deeper poverty
while still experiencing discrimination. Although the
New Deal tried to help farmers through the
Agricultural Adjustment Administration, which paid
farmers to cut back production and cease farming
parcels of land, it did little to improve the fortunes of
black tenant farmers and sharecroppers, who were
often forced off their plots to reduce production. In
this excerpt from an article in the NAACP's *Crisis*,
John P. Davis criticizes the New Deal's approach to
solving the problems of African American farmers in
the South.

The Agricultural Adjustment Administration
has used cruder methods in enforcing
poverty on the Negro farm population. It has
made violations of the rights of tenants under crop
reduction contracts easy; it has rendered
enforcement of these rights impossible. The
reduction of the acreage under cultivation through
the government rental agreement rendered
unnecessary large numbers of tenants and farm
laborers. Although the contract with the government
provided that the land owner should not reduce the
number of his tenants, he did so. . . . Farm laborers
are now jobless by the hundreds of thousands, the
conservative government estimate of the decline in
agricultural employment for the year 1934 alone
being a quarter of a million. The larger portion of
these are unskilled Negro agricultural workers—now
without income and unable to secure work or relief.

But the unemployment and tenant evictions
occasioned by the crop reductions policy of the
A.A.A. is not all. For the tenants and sharecroppers
who were retained on the plantations the

**749**

government's agricultural program meant reduced income. Wholesale fraud on tenants in the payment of parity checks occurred. Tenants complaining to the Department of Agriculture in Washington have their letters referred back to the locality in which they live and trouble of serious nature often results. Even when this does not happen, the tenant fails to get his check. The remainder of the land he tills on shares with his landlord brings him only the most meagre necessities during the crop season varying from three to five months. The rest of the period for him and his family is one of "root hog or die."

Source: John P. Davis, "A Black Inventory of the New Deal," *Crisis*, May 1935, 141–42.

## Document 22.7

### A Sharecropper's Family in Washington County, Arkansas, 1935

The Resettlement Administration (later the Farm Security Administration) documented the plight of migrant farmworkers and sharecroppers in numerous photographs. The following photo, taken by the noted photojournalist Arthur Rothstein, depicts a sharecropper's wife and daughters in Washington County, Arkansas, in 1935.

Franklin D. Roosevelt Library

## Document 22.8

### Martin Torres | Protest Against Maltreatment of Mexican Laborers in California, 1934

While union organizers achieved some gains in the industrial sector, they made little headway in the agricultural fields of California despite guarantees from the National Recovery Administration. In 1934 a delegation from the Confederation of Unions of Mexican Laborers and Peasants in the State of California attended a convention of workers in Mexico and asked for assistance. In response the Mexican organization (the Mexican Regional Confederation of Labor) sent the following letter to Josephus Daniels, the U.S. ambassador to Mexico.

Several months ago ten thousand compatriots in Southern California went on a strike. . . . These compatriots had been receiving ten cents per hour and were demanding thirty and that the children who had been working for five cents should be confined in future only to scholastic labors. The rich farmers of the region were not satisfied; they armed themselves to the teeth and taking advantage of a meeting which was being held by the strikers in the town of V[i]salia, they fired their guns on them, killing two, including a Mexican who, as a member of the Honorary Commission of a nearby town, was engaged in an investigation for the Government of Mexico. The farmer assassins fled. Later, they were tried by jury and were declared free of responsibility in the crime, and in order to celebrate, the following night an orgy was held which lasted till dawn and during which could be heard only the cry of "down with the Mexican greasers!" . . .

For months five thousand Mexicans in the Imperial Valley, California, have been on strike, and under the pretext of their upholding radical ideas, notwithstanding the fact that the N.R.A. has backed the strike, they have been treated worse than beasts by the authorities and farmers. They have been incarcerated, struck, fired upon, put out of their homes with their women and children with clubs, firearms and tear bombs, and many leaders are still under arrest in the prisons of that region. . . .

The Mexican Regional Confederation of Labor consider that the acts which motivated the complaints presented by our compatriots at the XI Convention of our Organization are radically opposed to the liberal purposes of the Honorable President—Mr. Franklin D. Roosevelt—which purposes he has publicly set forth on more than one occasion, and which he has crystallized into action, in some of his principles of Government so faithfully interpreted by you as Ambassador of that Democratic Administration, setting them forth in various addresses which you have made.

[Signed] Martin Torres, April 10, 1934

Source: "Protest Against Maltreatment of Mexican Laborers in California. General Secretary Martin Torres of Mexican Regional Confederation of Labor to United States Ambassador Josephus Daniels," April 20, 1934, in *Decade of Betrayal: Mexican Repatriation in the 1930s*, by Francisco E. Balderrama and Raymond Rodríguez (Albuquerque: University of New Mexico Press, 1995), 65–68.

Document 22.9

## Otis Nation | Testimony to the Great Plains Committee, 1937

In 1936 President Roosevelt established the Great Plains Committee to investigate the causes of the Dust Bowl and possible solutions for the region. The committee's report, submitted the following year, outlined how federal, state, and local government agencies could work together to restore the Great Plains to economic health. One of the witnesses the committee called to testify was Otis Nation, an organizer for the Oklahoma Tenant Farmers' Union, whose testimony follows.

Much has been written of our droughts here in Oklahoma, and how they have driven the farmers from the land. But little has been said of the other tentacles that choke off the livelihood of the small owner and the tenant. We do not wish to minimize the seriousness of these droughts and their effects on the farming population. But droughts alone would not have permanently displaced these farmers. The great majority of migrants had already become share-tenants and sharecroppers. The droughts hastened a process that had already begun. We submit the following as the cases for migratory agricultural workers:

1. *High interest rates.* Often a farmer borrows money for periods of 10 months and is charged an interest rate of 10 percent. These rates are charged when crops are good and when they fail. Through such practices the farmer loses his ownership; he becomes a tenant, then a sharecropper, then a migrant.
2. *The tenant and sharecropping system.* When share tenants are charged 33 1/3 percent of all corn or feed crops and 25 percent or more on cotton, plus 10 percent on all money borrowed at the bank, when sharecroppers are charged 50 to 75 percent of all he produces to the landlords, plus 10 percent for the bank's share on money invested; when these robbing practices are carried on in a community or a State, is it surprising that 33,241 farm families have left Oklahoma in the past 5 years?
3. *Land exhaustion, droughts, soil erosion, and the one-crop system of farming.* Lacking capital and equipment, small farmers have been unable to terrace their land or conduct other soil-conservation practices. The tenant and sharecropping system is chiefly responsible for the one-crop system. The landlord dictates what crops are to be planted—invariably cotton—and the tenant either plants it or gets off.
4. *Unstable markets.* Approximately a month and a half before the wheat harvest this year the price for this product was 93 cents here in Oklahoma City. But at harvest time the farmer sold his wheat for 46 cents to 60 cents per bushel, depending on the grade. . . . Kaffir [a grain sorghum] was selling

for $1.30 one month ago, and yesterday we sold some for 85 cents per hundred. . . .

It is obvious to all of us that farm prices are set by speculators. The farmer's losses at the market have contributed in no small part to the farmer losing his place on the land. Higher prices for farm products are quoted when the farmer has nothing to sell.

5. *Tractor farming.* In Creek County, Okla., we have the record of one land-owner purchasing 3 tractors and forcing 31 of his 34 tenants and croppers from the land. Most of these families left the State when neither jobs nor relief could be secured. This is over 10 families per machine, 10 families who must quit their profession and seek employment in an unfriendly, industrialized farming section of Arizona or California. Many of these families were even unable to become

"Joads" [the fictional family in *The Grapes of Wrath*] in these other States, and had to seek relief from an unfriendly national administration and a more unfriendly State administration. . . .

. . . There are no more important problems facing us than the problem of stopping this human erosion and rehabilitating those unfortunates who have already been thrown off the land. Certainly it is un-American for Americans to be starved and dispossessed of their homes in our land of plenty. Those who seek to exploit and harass these American refugees, the migratory workers, are against our principles of democracy.

Source: U.S. Congress, House Select Committee to Investigate the Interstate Migration of Destitute Citizens (Washington, DC: U.S. Government Printing Office, 1940–1941), 2102.

## Interpret the Evidence

1. What does Ann Marie Low's description of a typical day suggest about the particular challenges women faced during the Dust Bowl era (Document 22.5)?

2. According to John P. Davis (Document 22.6), why did the New Deal's AAA fail to help black farmers? How much of the problem was structural and how much resulted from racial prejudice?

3. In the photograph of the Arkansas family (Document 22.7), how do the subjects seem to react to the Great Depression? Compare their plight to that of black sharecroppers.

4. Why did unions in Mexico believe that Mexican farmworkers in California would receive assistance from the federal government (Document 22.8)? Compare their assumptions with Davis's (Document 22.6).

5. According to the Great Plains Committee testimony (Document 22.9), what role did human-caused factors play in producing the misery that accompanied the dust storms of the early 1930s?

## Put It in Context

What do these documents tell us about the challenges rural Americans faced during the Great Depression and their expectations regarding government help?